on the Romantic Age. Readers will come away from Birzer's subtle arguments better equipped to spot the use and abuse of history."

—Gleaves Whitney, director of Grand Valley State University's Hauenstein Center for Presidential Studies

"I'm not an Andrew Jackson fan, but I'm definitely a Bradley Birzer fan. His case for Old Hickory is as strong as any I've seen and deserves to be reckoned with."

—Thomas E. Woods Jr., author of *The Politically Incorrect Guide® to American History*

In Defense of Andrew Jackson

In Defense *of* Andrew Jackson

Bradley J. Birzer

REGNERY
HISTORY

Regnery History™ is a trademark of Salem Communications Holding Corporation
Regnery® is a registered trademark of Salem Communications Holding Corporation

Cataloging-in-Publication data on file with the Library of Congress

ISBN 978-1-62157-728-7
e-book ISBN 978-1-62157-843-7

Published in the United States by
Regnery History
An Imprint of Regnery Publishing
A Division of Salem Media Group
300 New Jersey Ave NW
Washington, DC 20001
www.RegneryHistory.com

Manufactured in the United States of America

10 9 8 7 6 5 4 3 2 1

Books are available in quantity for promotional or premium use. For information on discounts and terms, please visit our website: www.Regnery.com.

Contents

Foreword

I believe a biographer needs to see the world through the eyes of his or her subject. Though I've regularly taught college courses on the Jacksonian period of American history, 1807 to 1848, for two decades, I initially had reservations about throwing myself into the life, mind, and heart of Andrew Jackson. How could I—a central Kansas native and rather mild-mannered academic of German-Russian ancestry—understand this passionate and violent man of Scotch-Irish ancestry? Born exactly two hundred years before my own birth, Jackson seemed irreversibly removed from anything within my immediate experience, especially in his roles as a duelist, general, and U.S. president.

In the end, Jackson made bridging the gap between our worlds easy because whatever his faults—and there were many—he was nothing if not brutally honest about himself and his ideas. Endowed with a nearly supernatural will power and a conviction that could move mountains, Jackson considered it a virtue to be as consistent as possible, even in his violence. Throughout my research, I found evidence of his impressive dedication to this virtue, especially when examining Jackson's reveling in love, life, and his beliefs.

Still, I could never have written this book without the aid and encouragement of several friends. It was John J. Miller of *National Review* who recommended me as a potential author to the brilliant Harry Crocker, vice president and executive editor of Regnery Publishing. John has been a great ally and friend for more than a decade, and I consider him to be one of the finest writers of our era. My department chair and close friend, Mark Kalthoff, responded with immense enthusiasm when I mentioned the project to him. As is typical, we joked a bit before jumping into a serious historical conversation about Jackson and his era. Equally enthusiastic was another colleague and close friend, Paul Moreno, who immediately offered to read every word of the manuscript.

Science-fiction master Kevin J. Anderson told me that a writer should never turn down a challenge or a request—so when this one came along, I jumped at the chance. I wrote most of this book nearly 10,000 feet above sea level in a part of the country that would not officially become part of the United States until three years after President Jackson's death. Still, I think he would have approved of what I wrote.

Dan McCarthy, as always, offered me a number of insights on the Old Republicans and Larry White's excellent lectures on Jacksonian economics, which I attended in the early 1990s. Those lectures helped shape this book and still inform my view of the world.

I would also like to thank a number of other folks who provided encouragement and aid in one way or another: Winston Elliott, Gleaves Whitney, and Stephen Klugewicz at the *Imaginative Conservative;* Tom Woods at Liberty Classroom; Johnny Burtka and Bob Merry at the *American Conservative;* Tad Wert and Steve Babb, each from Tennessee; Kevin McCormick; Steve Horwitz; Sarah Skwire; my student research assistants, Scott Lowery and Hannah Socolofsky; Alex Novak, associate publisher of Regnery History; and Elizabeth Steger, my project editor at Regnery Publishing.

Two English, progressive rockers, Greg Spawton of Big Big Train and Robin Armstrong of Cosmograf, provided the soundtrack for the writing of this book. Most assuredly, President Jackson would not have approved of their contribution to it.

My greatest thanks, however, goes to my wife, Dedra McDonald Birzer, the wisest and most beautiful person I know. We spent countless hours during the composition of this book talking about history, biography, republicanism, heroism, integrity, character, grammar, style. . .and just about everything imaginable under the Colorado sun. Our kids—Nathaniel, Gretchen, Maria Grace, Harry, John Augustine, and Veronica Rose—gave us the space to talk, think, and write. John (age nine) even went so far as to write his own book, modeled after this one, chapter by chapter. Though instead of a biography of Andrew Jackson, he wrote a Tolkienian story about elves and faeries off on wacky and fascinating adventures. Jackson, of course, would not have approved.

Note on Sources

Throughout my research for this book, I have relied heavily on Jackson's writings. Jackson was an honest person, but he was a notoriously terrible speller. I have quoted him verbatim, misspellings and all. Whenever possible, I have followed the letters as printed in the *Correspondence of Andrew Jackson*, published by the Carnegie Institute of Washington, and *The Papers of Andrew Jackson*, published by the University of Tennessee Press. I have also leaned heavily on newspaper accounts, particularly those available at https://newspaperarchive.com, which were an indispensable resource. During my research, I was constantly surprised by how obsessed the London papers were with Jackson. The English view of Jackson would make a great and entertaining book, but it is beyond the scope of this one. Still, I have tried to incorporate the London papers wherever possible.

For readers who want to learn more about Jackson's life, *The Papers of Andrew Jackson* is an excellent, multi-volume source with helpful notes. Not only are the volumes of the highest quality in terms of publishing, print, and paper, I also found the editors' notes, annotations, interpretations, and marginalia to be of the highest order. Frankly, these volumes tell the story of Jackson's life far better than any biography yet written.

Note on Topics

In my professional career, I have had the great privilege of writing about men I admire, sometimes to the point of error: J. R. R. Tolkien; Charles Carroll of Carrollton; Christopher Dawson; Neil Peart; Russell Kirk; and, currently (after Jackson), Robert Nisbet. Of these subjects, I believe I could understand and explain the views of all but Charles Carroll because, as much as I love the man, Carroll's aristocratic intellect and temperament make him inaccessible to me.

This book is as much a biographical essay as it is a biography. Though brief, it was modeled after two of my favorite biographical essays, Russell Kirk's *John Randolph of Roanoke: A Study in American Politics* (1951) and Richard Brookhiser's *Founding Father: Rediscovering George Washington* (1997). Like Brookhiser and Kirk, I have done my best to get to know my subject—which was relatively easy because Andrew Jackson was so frank—and to reintroduce him to a new generation of readers. If Jackson read this account, I do not think he would challenge me to a duel—and once you read about him, you will realize that this might be the highest praise a biographer can earn.

My account of Andrew Jackson might not be the man in detail, but I hope that in its own way it offers the man in full.

Bradley J. Birzer
South Park, Colorado
May 11, 2018

Chapter One

Andrew Jackson and His Meaning to America

Washington, D.C., had never seen anything like it: close to 30,000 adorers of the president-elect poured into the area on the days preceding the inauguration, filling up every hotel and, seemingly, every nook and cranny of that swampy city. They "crowded" not only D.C. but also Arlington, Georgetown, and Alexandria with "carriages of every description, from the splendid Barronet and coach, down to wagons and carts, filled with women and children, some in finery, some in rags."[1] Everywhere, Jackson supporters glowed with enthusiasm. "Strange faces filled every public place, and every face seemed to bear defiance on its brow," one witness remembered.[2] Most had come from the West and the South, all eager to see Jackson, "the Servant" in the "presence of his Sovereign, the People."[3]

Jackson was a westerner, a war hero, an Indian fighter, a self-made man, a plain-spoken republican, and, unlike his six predecessors—four from the Virginia and two from the Massachusetts elite—not classically educated. In some ways, he was the first truly *American* president—not shaped by British manners and mores but something unique to this continent.

The weather rose to the occasion. Inauguration day, March 4, 1829, had started out "damp and cold" before becoming a "delightful and balmy day, with a clear sunshine and a soft southwest wind."[4] As the people approached the White House to witness the momentous event, they filled the streets and greenways and stood on every balcony, portico, and terrace.[5] They had been streaming into Washington for days, much to the delight and horror of many observers. As one not wholly unsympathetic senator noted, here was a manifestation of the god "De[i]mos" in all of his majesty and terror.[6]

While gratified by the crowd's enthusiasm, General Andrew Jackson felt a tinge of melancholy. His beloved wife Rachel had passed away suddenly, only four months earlier. She had died knowing that her husband had been elected president. But for Jackson, he had lost his closest adviser and confidante, one who had been with him through his more than thirty years of public service.[7]

Wearing a suit of unadorned black cloth, still in mourning for Rachel, General Andrew Jackson walked from Brown's Hotel to Gadsby's Hotel, where he was honored by a group of Revolutionary War veterans. He looked old and tired—his friends said he had aged twenty years in the last four months—and his journey from The Hermitage in Tennessee to Washington both inspired and exhausted him. Everywhere he stopped on that journey, which he had started in January, he heard proclamations of "Hurrah for Jackson." Every Ohioan, it was claimed, had shown up in Cincinnati to see the president-elect and so allegedly had every Pennsylvanian as he passed through Pittsburgh.[8]

William Polk, the leader of the veterans gathered at Gadsby's, offered his praise of the soon-to-be president. "We have entire confidence that the exercise of the same transcendent virtues [that were to be found in George Washington], will, under God, preserve inviolate our liberties, independence and union, during your administration," Polk proclaimed, and, "like your first predecessor, may you add a civic monument to your martial glory; and like his, may they be imperishable."[9] Jackson, himself a veteran of the Revolutionary War, responded that on his inauguration day, he could think of no better companions than those who had fought under Washington.

At eleven that morning, officers who had served under him at the 1815 Battle of New Orleans saluted Jackson in a similar ceremony. These men escorted President-elect Jackson to the Senate. He entered that chamber at 11:30 a.m., joined by U.S. congressmen, delegates, and ambassadors from foreign countries, and spectators fortunate enough to arrive in time to crowd into the room. Many of his admirers noted how republican Jackson looked in his plain clothes, standing straight, "crowned" by his dignified grey hair, while the foreigners looked buffoonish in their capes and official regalia. "Where lives the American who does not rejoice in the contrast," asked the *United States Telegraph*.[10] The whole event of the inaugural put the Europeans to shame, Washington resident Margaret Bayard Smith thought. "Even Europeans might have acknowledged that a free people, collected in their might, silent and tranquil, restrained solely by moral power without a shadow around of military force, was majesty, rising to sublimity, and far surpassing the majesty of Kings and Princes, surrounded with armies and glittering in gold."[11] Americans were keen to distinguish their manners and institutions from those of Europe. They believed America harkened back to democratic Greece and republican Rome while also establishing a model for the future of the world. John Adams voiced a common sentiment when he wrote in 1765, "I always consider the settlement of America with reverence and wonder, as the opening of a grand scene and design in Providence for the illumination of the ignorant, and the emancipation of the slavish part of mankind all over the earth."[12]

At high noon on inauguration day, cannons boomed across the D.C. skies, and Andrew Jackson walked out of the Capitol Rotunda and onto the platform where he was to speak. The 30,000 witnesses cheered so loudly that all other noise was drowned out.[13] Even throughout the wild applause, though, some telling sentences could be distinguished. "There is the old man and his gray hair." "There is the old veteran." "There is Jackson."[14] Then a deep and utter silence swept the mass of spectators as Jackson made a motion to indicate the beginning of his speech. The Tennessean bowed to the people, acknowledging them as the true source of sovereignty. His address, which was strong on principles if short on specifics, will never be remembered as one of the great presidential speeches, but it was revealing of the man.

Jackson thanked the American people for electing him their president and promised to uphold the Constitution, to approve public works only if they were constitutionally acceptable, to limit government spending and extinguish the national debt, to give preference to the militia rather than to a standing army, and to follow a "just and liberal policy" toward the American Indians. Perhaps most importantly, Jackson promised *reform* as an essential part of his first administration.[15] Reform, he said, "will require, particularly, the correction of those abusers" who have used "patronage" to put power in "unfaithful or incompetent hands."[16] The need to reform a corrupt federal government had been a consistent, and popular, theme of Jackson's campaign.

When he concluded his remarks, Jackson turned to the chief justice of the Supreme Court, John Marshall, and his attendants. One extended a Bible, and Jackson took the oath of office. Then Jackson took the Bible, kissed it, and bowed once more to "the people," who erupted into deafening cheers and applause.

Of that day, Margaret Bayard, one of the most important observers of Washington happenings in the first half of the nineteenth century, noted, "It was not a thing of detail [or] of a succession of small incidents. No, it was one grand whole, an imposing and majestic spectacle and to a reflective mind one of moral sublimity." Absent of any class, racial, or educational distinctions, 30,000 Americans surrounded the Capitol. Before actually catching sight of Andrew Jackson, they were "silent, orderly, and tranquil" with their eyes fixed on the front of the Capitol.[17] But then, almost as soon as Jackson finished his speech, the crowd turned into a mob, rushing to shake Jackson's hand and congratulate him. In doing so, Bayard wrote, they "nearly pressed him to death," and he was almost "suffocated and torn to pieces by the people." What degeneration, she gasped. "The Majesty of the People had disappeared, and a rabble, a mob, of boys, negros, women, children, scrambling, fighting, romping. What a pity what a pity! No arrangements had been made no police officers placed on duty and the whole house had been inundated by the rabble."[18] Another witness thought the entire scene was reminiscent of the German invasion of the Roman Empire, a "tumultuous tide."[19] Supreme Court Justice Joseph Story stood near Jackson. He wrote to his wife, "After the ceremony was over, the President went to the palace to receive company, and there he was visited by immense crowds of all sorts of people, from the highest and most polished down to the most vulgar and gross in the nation. I never saw such a mixture. The reign of 'King Mob' seemed triumphant."[20] Ever since, "King Mob" has become shorthand for the mood of Jackson's inauguration.

The raucous crowd followed Jackson, who was mounted on a white horse, all the way to the White House and kept celebrating even after Jackson quietly escaped back to his hotel to be alone with his thoughts. At the White House, the mob's muddy boots trampled the satin furniture, crowds knocked over huge barrels of orange punch and other refreshments, and, in desperation to clear the building, the serving staff moved the food and drink to the outside lawn.[21]

Congressmen and bureaucrats, upstanding or corrupt, all wondered what Jackson's election, a veritable democratic revolution, portended. Would the charismatic general and newly elected president overturn the Constitution, as some feared he would as the leader of a frontier mob, or would he fulfill it, as he, the good republican, had promised?

—

The key words of the Jacksonian era were "progress," "destiny," and "individualism"—a word that came into common usage in 1827. And what individuals they had then—not just remnants of the founders like John Adams, Thomas Jefferson, James Madison, and James Monroe—but what we might think of as the "new" Americans: John Quincy Adams, John C. Calhoun, Nathaniel Hawthorne, Catharine Beecher, James Fenimore

Cooper, Lucretia Mott, Frederick Douglass, Washington Irving, John Ross, Edgar Allen Poe, Susan B. Anthony, Moses Austin, Samuel Morse, Denmark Vesey, Elizabeth Cady Stanton, Francis Asbury, David Walker, John Taylor of Caroline, Daniel Webster, Cyrus McCormick, Brigham Young, Ralph Waldo Emerson, Black Hawk, Margaret Fuller, Henry David Thoreau, Henry Clay, Joseph Smith, John Deere, John C. Frémont, Winfield Scott, Elizabeth Ann Seton, Amos Kendall, Davy Crockett, Nat Turner, Herman Melville, Martin Van Buren, Tecumseh, Nicholas Biddle, Jim Bridger, Francis Scott Key, Charles Grandison Finney, Robert Owen, Jedediah Smith, Sojourner Truth, Tenskwatawa (the Shawnee Prophet), Sam Houston, John Randolph of Roanoke, Daniel Boone, William Barret Travis, Lewis Cass, and Lyman Beecher to name just a few.

The new Americans, especially those on the frontier, were self-reliant, restless, violent, suspicious of community, and optimistic about the future, as witnessed by their truly astounding birth rates—a woman living on the frontier might easily give birth to a dozen live children. One congressman remarked of this procreative vigor:

> I invite you to go to the west, and visit one of our log
> cabins, and number its inmates. There you will find a
> strong, stout youth of eighteen, with his Better Half,
> just commencing the first struggles of independent life.
> Thirty years from that time, visit them again; and

instead of two, you will find in that same family twenty-two. That is what I call the American Multiplication Table.

The American Multiplication Table demonstrated that Americans—with their open spaces and ever-expanding frontier, their productive farms, and their need for labor (and love for children)—out-procreated every people in the world, past or present.[22]

Alexis de Tocqueville astutely observed that Americans, as individualists, create their own communities through their families. "Individualism," he wrote, "is a considered and peaceful sentiment that disposes each citizen to isolate himself from the mass of his fellows and to withdraw to the side with his family and his friends; so that, after thus creating a small society for his own use, he willingly abandons the large society to itself."[23]

America's population grew dramatically between 1775 and 1846, and very little of it came from immigration.[24] Immigrants, to be sure, arrived on American soil, but the last great migration of free peoples—the Scotch-Irish—had tailed off around 1775. The next great migration of free peoples—the Irish, Germans, and Scandinavians—would not begin until 1846. When he was secretary of state, John Quincy Adams captured the American mood when he noted, "The American Republic invites nobody to come. We will keep out nobody. Arrivals will suffer no disadvantages as aliens. But they can expect no advantages either.

Native-born and foreign-born face equal opportunities. What happens to them depends entirely on their individual ability and exertions and on good fortune." With the important exception of the Chinese Exclusion Act in the early 1880s and an informal agreement with the Japanese in 1905, there were no limits on who could take up residence in the United States in the nineteenth and early twentieth centuries. Larger immigration restrictions did not begin until 1921 and 1924. They were revised during the Great Society of President Lyndon Johnson and then altered again after the September 11, 2001, terrorist attacks. But for most of America's early history, this was a land of open borders. American settlers also considered other borders open borders, spilling over into territory claimed by Spain or France or Mexico or Indians. Jackson was the American settlers' champion.

Though Andrew and Rachel Jackson had no children of their own,[25] the seventh president's most ardent supporters were men who led the big families on the frontier.[26] He understood their "rugged individualism," their need for land, their battles with the Indians, and their resentment of and frustration with the eastern establishment in Washington they considered snobbish and corrupt. For these people, the violent, honest, mercurial Scotch-Irish frontiersman was their warrior, philosopher, and knight, a real-life Natty Bumppo.

For much of the nineteenth century, Jackson stood as the great symbol of American democratic achievement—a man who came from the common people and represented them in the White

House. The Democratic Party treasured its heritage as the party of Jefferson and Jackson. Republicans, too, could cheer Jackson as the patriot who preserved the Union when South Carolina nullified a federal law in the 1830s. What if the mighty and honest Andrew Jackson, rather than the effete and deceptive James Buchanan, had been president when South Carolina again threatened to secede in December 1860? Almost certainly, the Civil War would have been prevented or, at the very least, postponed.[27]

Jackson was a giant American hero, celebrated in books throughout the nineteenth century. The two most important were written by James Parton and William Graham Sumner. To Parton, Jackson "was the most American of Americans—an embodied Declaration-of-Independence—the Fourth-of-July incarnate!"[28] Parton's sentiments were shared by most Americans at the time, whatever their personal political views.

But there were always skeptics, too. Prominent among them was William Graham Sumner (1840–1910). A professor of sociology at Yale, the most potent classical liberal of his day, and an anti-imperialist, Sumner approved of Jackson's limited government philosophy while still finding much to dislike in Jackson, the uncouth and bloody Celt from the backwoods. And it was this criticism that gained traction among some American intellectuals in the twentieth century.

The greatest American, conservative philosopher of the first half of the twentieth century, for instance, Harvard's Irving Babbitt, viewed Jackson as a symbol of all that was wrong with the republic. "The 'quality' in the older sense of the word suffered its first decisive defeat in 1829 when Washington was invaded by the hungry hordes of Andrew Jackson," Babbitt lamented. "The imperialism latent in this type of democracy appears in the Jacksonian maxim: 'To the victors belong the spoils.'" Babbitt's most famous student, T. S. Eliot, a New Englander raised in St. Louis who became a British national in the 1920s, echoed his teacher when he claimed that America had fallen when John Quincy Adams left the White House in 1829. There had only been six legitimate presidents in the United States, Eliot thought. Number seven could claim nothing—at least nothing good. Indeed, Eliot went so far as to call Jackson "abominable."[29]

But while some conservatives rejected Jackson, New Deal liberals, in one of the stranger twists of American intellectual history, rushed to embrace him, even though Jackson was an economic libertarian who would have found the New Deal unsound and dangerous to constitutional liberty. In 1945, Arthur Schlesinger Jr., who later became John F. Kennedy's court historian, published his most important and influential book *The Age of Jackson*, which became the touchstone of mainstream and liberal interpretations of President Jackson for the next two decades. Schlesinger used Jackson to justify a strong executive representing the will of the people, making him a sort of early precursor of Franklin Roosevelt.

In the 1960s, though, views of Jackson changed again—or there became two violently contrasting views. Academic Marxists regarded Jackson as a symbol of bloodthirsty capitalism and imperialism and his treatment of the American Indians as an example of hateful white supremacy. The mainstream view was maintained by the most important Jackson scholar of the twentieth century, Robert V. Remini, who praised Jackson as the president of the common man and a hero, even if an imperfect one.

Jackson found another champion in Paul Johnson, an English popular historian, public intellectual, and conservative journalist. Johnson's magisterial 1991 book, *The Birth of the Modern*, singles out Jackson's stunning victory at the Battle of New Orleans in 1815 as the beginning of the modern world and, ironically, the start of "the special relationship" between the United States and Britain in which the British Empire finally began to respect its former colonies. Jackson ushered in the democratic age because, as Johnson wrote, he "was instinctively a democrat.... He thought the people were instinctively right and moral, and Big Government, of the kind he could see growing up in Washington, instinctively immoral. His task was to liberate and represent that huge, most popular force by appealing to it over the oligarchic heads of the ruling elite. Here was a winning strategy, provided the suffrage was wide enough." As Jackson himself said, "The great constitutional corrective in the hands of the people against the usurpation of power, or corruption by their agents, is the right of suffrage; and this when used with calmness and deliberation will prove strong enough—it will perpetuate their liberties and rights."[30] Here again was Jackson as the great democrat. But a different view was in the ascendant—one that saw Jackson's flaws as far greater than his virtues.

In 2007, famed historian Daniel Walker Howe won the Pulitzer Prize for his book *What Hath God Wrought: The Transformation of America, 1815–1848*, (Volume 5 in the multi-volume *Oxford History of the United States*), in which he took Andrew Jackson, the Jacksonians, and the Democratic Party to task. Tellingly, Howe dedicates his work to the "Spirit of John Quincy Adams," the last gentleman, at least in the nineteenth century, to sit in the Oval Office. Howe casts Andrew Jackson as the man most responsible for destroying the founders' vision of a virtuous republic. "Despite his bow, Jackson brought to his task a temperament suited to leadership rather than deference," Howe explains. "Although he invoked a democratic ideology, the new president had profoundly authoritarian instincts. Tall, ramrod straight, with piercing eyes and an air of command, the hero of New Orleans was not a man to be crossed."[31] Or, as Henry Clay said at the time, fully understanding the democratic mass appeal of the militaristic demagogue, "Beware how you give a fatal sanction, in this infant period of our republic, scarcely yet two score years old, to military insubordination [referring to Jackson's alleged insubordination in Florida, which he invaded without explicit orders to do so and de facto took the territory for the United States]. Remember that Greece had her Alexander, Rome her Caesar, England her Cromwell, France her Bonaparte."[32]

Howe argues that nothing mattered more to Jackson and his supporters than the forced removal of the Indians. "Seeking the fundamental impulse behind Jacksonian Democracy, historians have variously pointed to free enterprise, manhood suffrage, the labor movement, and resistance to the market economy. But in its origins, Jacksonian Democracy.... as not primarily about any of these, though it came to intersect with all of them in due course. In the first place, it was about the extension of white supremacy across the North American continent.... And a statistical analysis of congressional behavior has found that....voting on Indian affairs proved to the most consistent predictor of partisan affiliation."[33] Ultimately, Howe concludes, "White supremacy, resolute and explicit, constituted an essential component of what contemporaries called 'The Democracy'—that is, the Democratic Party."[34]

Such criticisms, however, were ignored by the forty-fifth president of the United States, Donald J. Trump, who, like Ronald Reagan before him, was an admirer of Jackson and placed Jackson's portrait in the Oval Office. In March 2017, at an event celebrating the 250th anniversary of Jackson's birth, President Trump praised Jackson for acting "with courage, with grit, and with patriotic heart. And, by the way, he was one of our great Presidents." Trump continued:

> The political class in Washington had good reason to fear Jackson's great triumph. "The rich and powerful,"

Jackson said, "too often bend the acts of government to their selfish purposes." Jackson warned they had turned government into an "engine for the support of the few at the expense of the many."

Andrew Jackson was the People's President, and his election came at a time when the vote was finally being extended to those who did not own property. To clean out the bureaucracy, Jackson removed 10 percent of the federal workforce. He launched a campaign to sweep out government corruption. Totally. He didn't want government corruption. He expanded benefits for veterans. He battled the centralized financial power that bought influence at our citizens' expense. He imposed tariffs on foreign countries to protect American workers.

Trump then added, "That sounds very familiar," comparing Jackson's platform to his own.[35]

Following Trump's adulatory speech about Jackson, Robert Merry, the editor of the *American Conservative* and a well-respected American historian, wrote, "Andrew Jackson helped shape a political philosophy that has rippled through the American political firmament for nearly 200 years. Call it conservative populism—an aversion to bigness in all of its forms, including big government, and a faith in the capacity of ordinary folks to understand and to act upon their own interests. Conservative populism includes a natural aversion to entrenched elites, who always fight back against conservative populists whenever they challenge elite power. Republicans of today who tout the leadership of the last great GOP president, Ronald Reagan, should know they are touting the 20th century's greatest exponent of Jackson-style populist politics."[36]

Merry also noted Jackson's falling popular fortunes with liberals and professional historians:

> Andrew Jackson, the seventh president, doesn't get much respect these days. The Obama administration last year announced unceremoniously that the Treasury Department would rip his visage from the face of the $20 bill, where it has resided since 1928. A *New York Times* writer, in reporting that action, referred to him as "a white man known as much for his persecution of Native Americans as for his war heroics and his advocacy for the common man." A recent C-SPAN poll of historians on presidential performance had Jackson ranked at No. 18, a five-notch drop since a previous C-SPAN poll just a few years ago. Indeed, when the first such poll of academics was published in *Life* magazine in 1948, Old Hickory ranked up there at No. 6, and a 1996 poll had him at No. 5. He was considered one of the greats or at least near-greats. But no more. Such are the vagaries of presidential reputation in an era of political correctness.[37]

Jackson might be unpopular now, but his continued significance, including as a hero to the current president of the United States, is exactly what this book hopes to explain. I do not wish to give everything away at the beginning, but I will open this book by acknowledging that the more I have studied Andrew Jackson, the more I have come to respect him. Forced to rank the U.S. presidents in terms of character, honesty, and effectiveness (regardless of political positions), I would rank him number four, after Washington, Lincoln, and Reagan, respectively.

Unlike the first six presidents, Jackson did not turn to Cicero, Cato, or Seneca, though he certainly respected Stoicism, nor did he turn to Aristotle or Livy to help him understand events. Instead, his points of reference were his understanding of the U.S. Constitution and the example of the Scottish patriot William Wallace. Later in life, he referred frequently—from a Presbyterian perspective—to the Old and New Testaments of the Bible. Always, however, he based his decisions on experience and instinct. He was a man of the frontier, self-made but appreciative of those who gave him their loyalty and support. He was, pure and simple, an American, and perhaps the conclusions we draw about Jackson can tell us something about how we think about the very essence of our republic.

Chapter Two

Republican Violence

Scotch-Irish Honor

Andrew Jackson's parents (Andrew and Elizabeth) and his two older brothers (Hugh and Robert) left the north of Ireland for America in 1765, part of the great Scotch-Irish wave of immigration to the thirteen colonies.[1] Rugged, independent, poor, violent, hardworking, and Presbyterian, the Jacksons, like most of their fellow Celts, settled in the American highlands.

Elizabeth gave birth to their third and final son, Andrew, on March 15, 1767, somewhere on the Carolina borderlands, two days after the unexpected death of her husband. She moved with her three boys to her invalid sister's house in the Lancaster

District of South Carolina, where she helped out as a nurse and household manager. Robert Remini suggests that Elizabeth, a deeply religious woman, hoped her youngest son might become a learned Presbyterian minister.[2] But ornery "little Andy, the mischief-loving son of good aunt Betty,"[3] never considered such a career. Elizabeth sent Andrew to the best schools in the area, not that it did much good.[4] At school, Andrew was respectful of younger students but a brawler amongst his peers and older students. There is good evidence that he excelled at sports, especially in track and field events, and there is equally good evidence, from his later writings, that he didn't do so well in spelling and composition.[5]

Jackson's formal education might have been lacking, but his moral education was not, reflecting, even exaggerating, Scotch-Irish norms. He was honest. He was brave. He admired sexual purity. He revered women as morally superior to men. He was utterly devoted to his mother, and, later, to his wife Rachel.[6] He regarded them as virtual saints, and their advice as near holy writ. Jackson remembered these as his mother's last words:

> Andrew, if I should not see you again, I wish you to remember and treasure up some things I have already said [to] you: in this world you will have to make your own way. To do that you must have friends. You can make friends by being honest, and you can keep them by being steadfast. You must keep in mind that

friends worth having will in the long run expect as much from you as they give to you. To forget an obligation or be ungrateful for a kindness is a base crime—not merely a fault or a sin but an actual crime. Men guilty of it sooner or later suffer the penalty. In personal conduct be always polite but never obsequious. None will respect you more than you respect yourself. Avoid quarrels as long as you can without yielding to imposition. But sustain your manhood always. Never bring a suit in law for assault and battery or for defamation. The law affords no remedy for such outrages that can satisfy the feelings of a true man. Never wound the feelings of others. Never brook wanton outrage upon your own feelings. If you ever have to vindicate your feelings or defend your honor, do it calmly. If angry at first, wait till your wrath cools before you proceed.[7]

This was the code of Scotch-Irish honor he learned from his mother and that he tried to live by—and there was a political component to it. Jackson remembered:

To the lessons she inculcated on the youthful minds of her sons, was, no doubt, owing, in a great measure, that fixed opposition to British tyranny and oppression, which afterwards so much distinguished them. Often she would spend the winter's evenings, in recounting to them the sufferings of their grandfather, at the siege of Carrickfergus, and the oppression exercised by the nobility of Ireland, over the labouring poor; impressing it upon them, as a first duty, to expend their lives, if it should become necessary, in defending and support the natural rights of men.[8]

By all accounts, Elizabeth Jackson was an impressive person—she certainly was to her son Andrew.

Later in life, Jackson advised that William Wallace, the medieval Scottish patriot, was the model by which young men should judge themselves. "In him we find a stubborn virtue, which was never overcome by vice, it was too pure for corruption," he wrote. "We find in him the truly undaunted courage, always ready to brave any dangers, for the relief of his country or his friend. In him we find true greatness of soul capable of true friendship, and in his enemies, a lesson from the want of it, necessary for every virtuous high minded youth to be acquainted with, that he may be guarded against the vile hypocrisy, & deceit, that often lurks beneath a fair exterior which is cloathed with power."[9] One of the best unsung historians of the Jacksonian period, Russell Kirk, argued that Sir Walter Scott was to blame for the South's culture of prideful "honor." But the Scotch-Irish didn't need inspiration from Scott; their belief in honor was passed down from remembered tradition and history.

That honor was put to the test in the American War of Independence, which, in the South, was a civil war with neighbors and even family members choosing rival sides. The Jacksons and the Crawfords (the family that sheltered the Jacksons) were patriots, who disdained British rule. Andrew's oldest brother, Hugh, joined a southern militia and died near Charleston, South Carolina, at the Battle of Stono Ferry on June 20, 1779.[10] The first battle near the Jackson home was the Battle of Hanging Rock, August 1, 1780. Andrew participated in the battle, though he was only thirteen years old. Most likely, he served as a scout and messenger for Colonel William R. Davie, a man Jackson admired immensely.[11] At one point, in the fall of 1780, he got so close to the infamous and brutal British Lieutenant Colonel Banastre Tarleton that he "could have shot him."[12] Though Jackson failed to shoot Tarleton, he did participate in a number of skirmishes against the British and Loyalists after this encounter. During one such protracted skirmish, the British captured Andrew, now fourteen, and his brother Robert. A British officer demanded that Andrew shine his boots, and when Andrew refused, the officer struck him savagely with his sword. "Andrew broke the force of the blow with his left hand, and thus received two wounds—one deep gash on his head, and another on his hands the marks of both of which he carried to his grave."[13] The scar was so severe that even as an adult, Jackson could place a full finger in it.[14] After striking Andrew, the officer turned his sword on Robert, wounding him horribly in the head. The British gave the boys little water or food, and, as Jackson remembered, "No attention whatever was paid to the wounds or to the comfort of the prisoners, and the small pox having broken out among them, for want of proper care, many fell victims to it. I frequently heard them groaning in the agonies of death and no regard was paid to them."[15]

No one ever treated Robert's head wounds, and both brothers contracted small pox.[16] Elizabeth Jackson worked diligently to secure the release of her two boys and five of their neighbors,[17] though even at his release, the British denied Andrew his jacket and shoes.[18] She nursed her sons as well as she could, but Robert died two days after reaching home, and Andrew suffered intensely for months to come. Once Andrew seemed well enough, Elizabeth went to Charleston to serve as a nurse and died there from "ship fever."[19]

Barely aged fourteen and still suffering the after-effects of small pox, Andrew Jackson had no family left. He owned no property, and he had no future. He was utterly alone. To write that he hated the British would be a gross understatement. He despised them. When his biographer James Parton interviewed some of Jackson's surviving friends, relatives, and neighbors for his 1860 biography of the man, one relative speculated on how much Jackson hated the British. "I'll warrant Andy thought of it at [the 1815 Battle of] New Orleans," he said.[20]

With the American War of Independence over (essentially in 1781, officially in 1783) and his family gone, Jackson lived first with an uncle and then with some distant relatives, and he worked,

briefly, as a saddler.[21] Unsatisfied, Jackson moved again, this time
to a school to finish his education. In 1784, he began to study law,
and he became a licensed attorney in North Carolina in 1787 and,
in 1788, in Tennessee.[22] Jackson made a striking impression. He
did not follow the fashion of wearing powdered wigs, but as one
woman remembered,

> [Jackson] had his abundant suit of dark red hair
> combed carefully back from his forehead and temples
> and, I suspect, made to lay down smooth with bear's-
> oil. He was full six feet tall and very slender, but yet of
> such straightness of form and such proud and graceful
> carriage as to make him look well proportioned. In
> feature he was by no means good-looking. His face was
> long and narrow, his features sharp and angular and
> his complexion yellow and freckled, but his eyes were
> handsome. They were very large, a kind of steel-blue,
> and when he talked to you he always looked straight
> into your own eyes. I have talked with him a great
> many times and never saw him avert his eyes from me
> for an instant. It was the same way with men.[23]

She also noted that he had two ways of talking. He could
speak calmly and reasonably, but if he got excited, he would suddenly express himself with a lingering northern Irish accent.
Regardless, she noted, he always possessed a "presence, or kind

of majesty."[24] And, of course, he was sensitive and prickly about his honor. During one court case, when he felt his opponent had treated him dishonorably, Jackson challenged him to a duel.

> Sir: When a man's feelings and charector are injured he ought to seek a speedy redress; you rec[eive]d, a few lines from me yesterday and undoubtedly you understand me. My charector you have injured; and further you have Insulted me in the presence of a court and larg audiance. I therefore call upon you as a gentleman to give me satisfaction for the Same; and I further call upon you to give Me an answer immediately without Equivocation and I hope you can do without dinner untill the business done; for it is consistent with the character of a gentleman when he Injures a man to make a spedy reparation; therefore I hope you will not fail in meeting me this day.[25]

The duel came to nothing, as each man simply shot into the air and walked away.[26]

Jackson lived by aphorisms and maxims. One of the most important was "for malicious Slander all men are answered at the Bar of honor."[27] True civilization, he believed, required ungrudging submission to such rules, which were his equivalent of natural law.[28] As a United States senator, Jackson witnessed two altercations on the House floor in the winter of 1798. Instead of settling matters definitively with pistols, the disputes dragged on and on with threats, arguments, and spit tobacco juice at "the expense of sixteen days spent in debating the subjects in the House of Representatives." It was, he feared, an immense "disgrace," costing the republic time, honor, and nearly $10,000. "This will serve for a specimen of Eastern quarrels," he commented.[29] Far better, for him, was the "western" way, with a pistol.

Despite his temper, or perhaps, in part, because of it, Jackson prospered as a lawyer and began to acquire property and establish himself as a southern gentleman.[30] By 1791, he was appointed a trustee of Davidson Academy, and in 1792 Tennessee commissioned him a judge advocate.[31]

Rachel: Jackson's Saint—and Scandal

Restless and ambitious, Jackson moved to Nashville in late 1788. There he met a woman described as gorgeous, spirited, and highly intelligent—indeed, Rachel Donelson Robards was highly regarded in Tennessee frontier society. Jackson boarded with her family. Mrs. Donelson (Rachel's mother and a widow—her husband had been murdered) ran a boarding house. Eventually, Jackson started courting Rachel, neither one of them knowing that she was still legally married to Lewis Robards, a Virginian living in Kentucky. Rachel and Lewis Robards had been married on March 1, 1785.[32] The marriage, however, was an unhappy one. The couple separated, and Rachel returned to her mother. In 1790, Robards sued for divorce, and Rachel assumed the divorce was final, though the legal process was never completed.[33] While Rachel was satisfied and relieved at her apparent divorce from Robards, he seethed with resentment and jealousy, slept with slave women, and plotted his revenge, which came in 1792 when he filed for divorce again, this time with "a charge of adultery exhibited against her."[34]

Jackson's extant letters reveal little about his courtship of Rachel, but apparently the couple eloped to Natchez and found a Roman Catholic priest who annulled Donelson's marriage to Robards (which suggests there were grounds to consider the union invalid)[35] and married them in the Catholic Church, though neither Jackson nor his wife were Catholic.[36] Whatever the exact circumstances, by October 1791, Andrew Jackson referred to Rachel as "Mrs. Jackson."[37] They were married again, in a Protestant ceremony, at the Donelson home in Nashville on January 17 or 18, 1794, with Rachel's divorce from her first husband now a settled matter of law, and to make sure there was no legal doubt about their own union (which had been first sealed in what was then Spanish Mississippi).[38] Unfortunately, for the rest of Jackson's public life, his marriage to Rachel Donelson remained a subject of gossip, innuendo, and outright lies. Every time Jackson stood for election, the press debated the issue again with a fierce partisan intensity, and books poured off presses raising the following question: "Ought a convicted adulteress and her paramour husband to be placed in the highest offices of this land?"[39]

On December 18, 1828, Rachel, an unwavering evangelical Christian, who generally ignored the gossip, found an anti-Jackson tract describing her supposed lewdness and "whorishness." She was shocked, mortally so, collapsing from a heart attack or stroke, and died three days later, giving Jackson even more reason to hate his scandalmongering enemies.

They had been a devoted couple. When they were separated, Jackson wrote to her frequently expressing sentiments similar to this:

> It is with greatest pleasure I sit down to write you. Tho I am absent My heart rests with you. With what pleasing hopes I view the future period when I shall be restored to your arms there to spend My days in Domestic Sweetness with you the Dear Companion of my life, never to be separated from you again during this Transitory and fluctuating life.
>
> I mean to retire from the Buss of publick life, and Spend My Time with you alone in Sweet Retirement, which is My only ambition and ultimate wish.…
>
> Could I only know you were contented and enjoyed Peace of Mind, what satisfaction it would afford me whilest travelling the loanly and tiresome road. It would relieve My anxious breast and shorten the way— May the great "I am" bless and protect you until that happy and wished for moment arrives when I am

restored to your sweet embrace which is the Nightly prayer of your affectionate husband, Andrew Jackson.[40]

To Jackson, Rachel was a moral exemplar, and, though few of her letters survive, it is clear that theirs was a union of mind as well as soul and body.[41]

Jackson's Rise

Despite the controversy about their marriage, the Jacksons moved up quickly in society. The city of Nashville appointed Jackson to the Tennessee Constitutional Convention in early 1796, and in October the state elected him to the House of Representatives. On December 8, three days after Jackson's arrival in Congress, President Washington gave his farewell address, which was censured by the Jeffersonians as too pro-British. Jackson voted with them.[42]

The Tennessee legislature elected Jackson to the United States Senate on October 19, 1797, and he entered the Senate on November 22.[43] His departure for the capital pained him deeply. "I must now beg of you to try to amuse Mrs. Jackson and prevent her from fretting," he wrote to a friend. "The situation in which I left her—(Bathed in Tears) fills me with woe. Indeed Sir, It has given me more pain than any Event of my life."[44]

As a senator, Jackson sided with the Jeffersonian Republicans against the Federalists. He thought the latter were too pro-British and too much in favor of centralized government. Jackson supported states' rights,[45] including a state's right to defend it citizens from Indian attacks.[46] He wanted the United States to avoid war with Britain and revolutionary France.[47] Jackson feared that in such a war the Indians would be allies of the Europeans, but he also argued for protecting Indians from unscrupulous whites.[48]

The most pressing issue for Jackson was supporting settlers in their frontier battles. The original thirteen states had been given the legal right to extinguish Indian land claims within their borders. Tennessee believed it had an equal right to do so under the Constitution.[49] Though many in Congress were unsympathetic to the settlers on the frontier, Jackson convinced the Senate to allow President John Adams to negotiate a new treaty with the Cherokees. He hoped it might take into account the settlers' grievances.[50] Jackson thought his eastern colleagues simply did not understand the settlers' hardships. "Those distress'd Citizens derive their Support, from the pursuits of agriculture alone, and Shou'd they [because of Indian raids] not be enabled to return to their farms, in time to make their Summer crops; they will be reduced to a most deplorable State," he argued.[51]

Though Jackson was an ardent Jeffersonian,[52] Jefferson did not think highly of him. In 1824, Jefferson told Daniel Webster that Jackson "could never speak" during his short career in the Senate "on account of the rashness of his feelings. I have seen him attempt it repeatedly, as often choked with rage." Jackson, he believed, was not only "most unfit" but also "dangerous."[53] Albert

Gallatin, Jefferson's secretary of the Treasury, possessed similar memories. Jackson, he thought, was nothing more than a "tall, lank, uncouth-looking personage, with long locks of hair hanging over his face, and a cue down his back tied in an eel-skin; his dress singular, his manners and deportment that of a rough backwoods-man."[54] As Gallatin watched Jackson's fame rise as a military hero, he came to fear Jackson even more, regarding him as a natural populist dictator.[55]

It is interesting, in that regard, that Jackson, for a time, supported Napoleon, hoping the French dictator might, like William the Conqueror, land French troops on English soil. "Should Boneparte [sic] make a landing on the English shore, Tyranny will be Humbled, a throne crushed, and a republick will spring from the wreck—and millions of distressed people restored to [the rights of man by the] conquering arm of [Bonaparte]."[56] While in the Senate, he voted against the purchase of cannon foundries (presumably for use against France) and a measure to arm merchant ships.[57] His support for Napoleon, however, was not without limits. Should France and Britain make a quick peace, he cautioned, Napoleon might very well turn his sights on reclaiming the abandoned French empire in North America.[58]

Part of Jackson's admiration for Napoleon came from his hatred of the British, but it also came from his opposition to President John Adams and the Federalists who were pro-British in their sympathies and partisan in their administration of government. Adams, he wrote, had dismissed "all those from office who differ from him in politicks," replacing them "with men who subscribe trully to all his acts."[59] He also strongly disapproved of Adams's use of the Alien and Sedition Acts to, in his view, stifle dissent.[60]

However strong his political views, Jackson disliked legislative life; he thought it consisted of too much talk, too much committee work, and too much increasing of the wealth of American officials at the expense of the country.[61] He had learned to distrust the national government as ignorant, arrogant, and self-serving. Jackson put his trust instead in the republican virtue of common people in local communities. Neither congressional life nor Philadelphia, the capital from December 6, 1790, to May 14, 1800, suited Jackson, and he resigned from his Senate seat in April 1798. He was profoundly homesick for Nashville and Rachel.[62] He returned to Tennessee where he was immediately appointed a judge of the Tennessee Superior Court, and, three years later, major general of the Tennessee militia. It was as major general of the Tennessee militia that Andrew Jackson finally became Andrew Jackson.

Gentleman Dueler

Jackson found being a judge about as uncongenial as being a congressman. "Sensibly alive to the difficult duties of this station, distrusting his legal acquirements, and impressed with the great injury he might produce to suitors, by erroneous decision, he advanced to the office with reluctance, and in a short time resigned," his first biographers John Reid and John Henry Eaton wrote, "leaving it open for those, who, he believed, were better qualified than himself, to discharge its intricate and important duties."[63]

Jackson instead devoted himself to honing the state militia and farming, building his plantation and manor house, The Hermitage.[64] For Jackson, however, private life did not necessarily mean a peaceful life, and, as such scholars as Grady McWhiney and Forrest McDonald have demonstrated, of all the ethnic and religious groups that settled in early America, none were so violent as the Scotch-Irish.[65] Jackson was equal parts a frontiersman, a republican (which meant, by duty, a citizen soldier), and Scotch-Irish.

No one knows exactly how many duels Jackson fought, but they were frequent and often made news. Duels were governed by informal but strictly enforced codes and rules. They were generally fought over accusations of cowardice or dishonesty or in defense of a woman or her family who had been insulted. Jackson avoided dueling with his social inferiors, either ignoring them or giving them a beating instead. Duels were matters of honor, fought to defend social standards. In a duel, a man demanded "satisfaction," which was met by the duelers simply meeting on the field and exchanging shots, not necessarily shooting their opponent. Missing on purpose was allowed, and afterward the men could even become friends. Among the most infamous of Jackson's duels were those with John Sevier in 1803, Charles

Dickinson in 1806, and Thomas Hart Benton's family in 1813. Though Jackson killed Dickinson, he reconciled with Sevier and especially with Thomas Hart Benton after their respective battles.

In 1803, Governor Sevier, a longtime political rival of Jackson's, confronted Jackson in a public square and accused him of adultery. He was retaliating for Jackson's friend, the previous governor, Archibald Roane, having accused him of profiting from political office. Jackson was furious and had to be restrained from attacking Sevier. They agreed to a duel but could not agree on a time or a place. Letters were exchanged to try to settle the arrangements. In Jackson's first letter to Sevier, dated October 2, 1803, he wrote:

> The ungentlemany Expressions, and gasgonading conduct, of yours relative to me on yesterday was in true character of your self, and unmask you to the world, and plainly shews that they were the ebulations of a base mind goaded with stubborn prooffs of fraud, and flowing from a source devoid of every refined sentiment, or delicate sensation. But sir the Voice of the people has made you a Governor. This alone makes you worthy of my notice or the notice of any Gentleman. To the office I bear respect, to the Voice of the people who placed it on you I pay respect, and as such I only deign to notice you, and call upon you for that satisfaction and explanation that your ungentlemany conduct & expressions

require, for this purpose I request an interview, and my friend who will hand you this will point out the time and place, when and where I shall Expected to see you with your friend and no other person. My friend and myself will be armed with pistols.[66]

The rules of southern dueling required each dueler to have a "second," not only to keep the two duelers honest but also to have a backup should the primary fall.

Sevier's response mocked Jackson and his challenge, imitating it almost word for word, but with better spelling:

Your Ungentlemanly and Gasgonading conduct of yesterday, and indeed at all other times heretofore, have unmasked yourself to me and to the World. The Voice of the Assembly has made you a Judge, and this alone has made you Worthy of My notice or Any other Gentleman, to the office I have respect and this Alone makes you worthy of my notice.[67]

Sevier concluded the letter, accepting any time or place named by Jackson but outside the state of Tennessee, where dueling was technically illegal. The men exchanged letters for more than a week. Jackson grew so frustrated with their inability to find a place and time to duel that he finally published a public announcement: "To all whom Shall See these presents Greeting—Know yea that I Andrew Jackson, do pronounce, Publish, and declare to the world, that his Excellency John Sevier Esqr. Governor, Captain General and commander in chief, of the land and Naval forces of the State of Tennessee—is a base coward and poltroon. He will basely insult, but has not the courage to repair the wound."[68] Finally, the two men agreed to duel at Southwest Point in Virginia. Jackson arrived early; Sevier arrived late. When Jackson saw Sevier approaching, he had an ally ride forward to deliver a letter to the governor, listing every crime the man had supposedly committed against Jackson. Sevier, though, refused to accept the letter, which threw Jackson into a rage. Jackson mounted his horse and charged Sevier, brandishing his cane as a weapon. Sevier fell off his horse, fumbling as he tried to unsheathe his sword. The sword broke as Sevier hit the ground. Jackson considered the matter done, and the men and their followers rode happily into town, friendly once again.[69]

The duel with Charles Dickinson, a lawyer and slave trader, did not end on such a jolly note. The reason for the duel remains unclear, but it probably involved an insult to Rachel[70] as well as competing bets on horse racing. The dispute became public, people took sides, and Jackson ended up beating an ally of Dickinson, Thomas Swann, a young lawyer who had recently arrived from Virginia, with a cane. Partisans for either side dueled, and on May 23, 1806, Jackson challenged his primary antagonist to a duel. "You have, to disturb my quiet, industriously excited Thomas Swann to quarrel with me, which involved the peace and harmony of society for a while," he wrote.[71] Dickinson and Jackson finally met on the morning of May 30, 1806. Immaculately dressed, they stood back to back. When the call was made, each walked eight paces and turned at the pegs that marked their respective firing lines. Dickinson fired first. His shot hit Jackson squarely in the chest. Dickinson fell back from his peg and was ordered to return to his position. He did. Jackson calmly aimed and fired, sending a lethal bullet through Dickinson's body, just below the ribs and above the hips.[72] Dickinson bled in intense agony for almost twenty-four hours before dying.[73] If Jackson thought the duel might end the fighting, he was wrong, even if the fighting moved to the newspapers.[74] The resulting controversy never went away and nearly cost Jackson his political career.

Jackson's duel with his friend Thomas Hart Benton happened during the War of 1812. In 1813, Benton traveled to Washington to defend his commander, Major General Andrew Jackson, from several false charges. While he was traveling, his younger brother Jesse got into a dispute with Tennessee politician William Carroll. Both men were serving under Jackson's command, and the general encouraged them to settle their differences peaceably. When instead Jackson was forced to choose sides in a duel, he stood as Carroll's second. Both men survived but were wounded, with Jesse Benton shot in the hip. Thomas Hart Benton blamed Jackson for failing to protect his brother. Jackson, in turn, felt betrayed by Thomas Hart Benton for not accepting that he had had good reason to side with Carroll. "Has any act of my life towards you since I took you by the hand in Friendship and appointed you my aid de Camp been inconsistent with the strictest principles of Friendship?" he asked.[75] Bewildered, Benton responded, "You had been my friend [and] I could not sit, and smile assent upon your cowardly act, which I saw you doing what you could to break the heart of an aged and widowed mother, and hurrying into his grave, a young man, a brother, whose life ought to have been preserved for the comfort of his family and the service of his country."[76] Jesse, of course, was very much alive, but Thomas Hart Benton made the point that that was through no effort of Jackson's.

After months of tension, challenges, and refusals, Jackson confronted the Benton brothers on September 4, 1813, at the City Hotel in Nashville. Accounts of the fight vary, and there were others involved. But we know shots were fired and knives were unsheathed. No one died in the fight, but Jackson was shot in the shoulder, the ball, embedded in the bone, staying there forever. While a doctor recommended amputation, Jackson refused, and the arm healed. Astoundingly, the law ignored the fight, and Benton immediately published an apology for the brawl. He and Jackson were not only reconciled but also became close political allies.[77] That was Andrew Jackson, the man of the frontier—no worse enemy, no better friend.

Chapter Three

Frontiersman, Citizen Soldier, and Hero

The aspects of Andrew Jackson's life that recent biographers have consistently overlooked are his motivations and role as a frontiersman. Most students of history tend to think of Jackson as a southerner. This is true, of course, but only partially. His South was the southern frontier, not the South of Old Virginia or the eastern shore of Maryland. And the same students usually don't know that Jackson's views about the frontier permeated his thoughts, policies, and desires. In fact, they justified (and helped explain) his violence and informed his hatred of the East, especially Washington, D.C.

Jackson saw himself as truly principled and viewed those on the East Coast as naïve. From the safety of Washington, Boston, or New York, they could wax poetic and philosophic about rights and peace and abuses committed against Indians while lambasting the actions of Americans settling in newly claimed territory. They could loiter in the halls of Congress or walk through New York's financial district while real Americans waged war on an untamed wilderness and protected their families from almost constant attack. From Jackson's point of view, most politicians and bankers simply lived off the work of those who were forging the country along the frontier lines. To him, two classes of Americans existed: those who labored and those who stole.

Whatever we think about the frontier and its place in American history, the same will be true of Jackson, the very embodiment of the old southwestern frontier. As far back as the 1820s and 1830s, prominent figures such as Washington Irving and James Fenimore Cooper wanted to know Jackson, not necessarily because they agreed with his policies but because they understood even during his lifetime what a mythic figure he was and would remain.[1] Currently, the nature of Jackson's legendary status is tied up in our twenty-first-century ideas about the frontier. If we consider forging a republic out of virgin soil a grand achievement in our nation's history, Jackson is a heroic pioneer. If we see our country's past as criminal and inhumane, an imperialist move justified for a corrupt understanding of republicanism, Jackson is a despicable savage. Either title has mythic proportions, but determining which one Jackson deserves is not easy because the true account of his life as a frontiersman may have become irretrievably corrupted.

A key reason pro-Jackson scholars have neglected Jackson's role as a frontiersman is that they do not want to delve too deeply into his Indian removal policy and the resultant Trail of Tears. Strangely enough, they can excuse his owning slaves as a cultural norm, but they feel differently about his views toward the American Indian. In stark contrast, the historians who hate Jackson—especially the New Leftists of the 1970s and 1980s—focus almost exclusively on his treatment of the Indians, but they rarely explain it in the context of his times or the contours of his rather nuanced thought when dealing with native peoples. To the New Left historians of the 1960s through today, Jackson's removal policy is incontrovertible proof of the evils of nineteenth-century, laissez-faire capitalism and its twin—freewheeling imperialism. In fact, according to the best of the New Left historians, Patricia Limerick, there is little left to understand and study about the West except the "legacy of conquest."[2]

The Citizen Soldier

Jackson, it is true, was a conqueror and a general, but that can be misleading. He was, more fundamentally, a republican, a defender of America as a democratic republic, and an advocate of the aggressive territorial expansion that republic was creating because, in Jefferson's famous phrase, it was an "empire of liberty."

Though a military man who believed in conquest to defend the United States and expand the republic, he opposed the idea of a standing army. He was well versed in the Anglo-Saxon common law tradition that warned standing armies were beholden only to the sovereign will of the British king (or the national executive power) rather than to the localities, local charters, and organic, common law that governed militias, making standing armies a potential threat to freedom.[3] Jackson was very much in the tradition of American men, stretching back to the colonial period, who thought of themselves as citizen soldiers with a right and duty to defend their communities. The same men regarded a standing army as a waste of a country's resources and a danger to its liberties. Even the experience of the War of 1812—which confirmed for many Americans the ineffectiveness of militias—did not change Jackson's mind. At his first inaugural, he had welcomed militias but wanted no national military participation.

In this, Jackson was a thoroughgoing conservative, if not a reactionary, because by 1816 many Americans were convinced that a modern, expanding American nation needed a national military. Jackson remained a lifelong skeptic of this view, but he reluctantly conceded that a standing army could have two legitimate constitutional responsibilities: enforcing treaties with the Indians (though, as a frontiersman, he accepted that settlers who moved beyond America's borders were responsible for their own defense) and defending the United States from European enemies.

When writing out his Independence Day toasts in 1805, Jackson, tellingly, toasted the militias before the army. "The Militia of the United States—the sure Bulwark of freedom." That was toast number seven. Toast number eleven was to the "Army of the united States," which he tempered with the following caveat: "may [the officer or soldier] never be doomed, to persecution and Tyranny under a government of laws to satiate the private spleen of a would be Despot."[4]

Five years later, explaining his position to the governor of Tennessee, Jackson wrote, "Our independence and Liberty was not obtained without expence—it was dearly Bought—both with Blood and Treasure, It must be preserved—the pence on this subject never could be counted—and its only real and substantial defence is a well organized militia," which he contrasted with the "corruption" manifest in "our regular army." This confirmed for Jackson that "the ideas contained in the constitution" were "verified."[5]

When young men volunteered for the militia, received training, and returned to civilian life, Jackson believed they would leaven the civic virtue of their fellow Americans.[6] In March 1812, Jackson, anticipating war with Britain, called for volunteers to join his militia. "No drafts or compulsory levies are now to be made. A simple invitation is given to the young men of the country to arm for their own and their countries rights." A republic, he believed, depended on the volunteer citizen soldier:

A nobler feeling should impell us to action. Who are
we? And for what are we going to fight? Are we the
titled Slaves of George the third? The military con-
scripts of Napolon [sic] the great? Or the frozen peas-
ants of the Russian Czar? No. We are the free born sons
of America, the citizens of the only republic now existing in the world; and the only people on Earth who
possess rights, liberties, and property which the[y] dare
call their own.[7]

During the War of 1812, when the army ordered Jackson's
militia to join its regular units, Jackson brazenly countermanded
the order, noting that as militia his volunteers could not legally be
drafted against their will. "Such patriots as I have the honor to
command that our country and its liberties are to be saved and
defended—that a well organized militia is the bulwark of our
Nation—I have no hesitation in giving the lie to the modern doctrine that it is inefficient to defend the liberties of our country, and
that standing armies are necessary—in time of peace."[8] When the
federal government lamented the supposed failures of the militias,
Jackson wrote a furious note to Secretary of War John Armstrong,
noting all the failures of the United States military, especially William Hull's 1812 surrender of the northwestern army of the United
States to the British at Detroit. Additionally, Jackson demanded,
how could such detractors of the militia not see that the entire
"barbarous" and "bloody" history of Europe demonstrated how

horrific standing armies were to liberty and stability. Those men who volunteer for militia duty are "the best materials on earth." Jackson thanked God that "the law under which they were raised [had] given them their arms until they choose to resign them."[9] These were the true patriots of America.

Empire of Liberty: The Louisiana Territory

Jackson saw no contradiction between his opposition to a large standing army and his wholehearted support for expanding the territorial dominion of the United States across the continent. In an effusive letter to President Thomas Jefferson after the United States purchased the Louisiana Territory from France, he wrote,

> We hope in the golden moment of American prosperity, when all the western Hemisphere rejoices in the Joyfull news of the Cession of Louisiana—an event which places the peace happiness and liberty of our country on a permanent basis, an event which generations yet unborn in each revolving year will hail the day and with the causes that gave it birth, such Joy as this we hope will not be interrupted.[10]

So great was Jackson's enthusiasm for the purchase that several friends petitioned President Jefferson to appoint him the first territorial governor. Representative George Washington Campbell of Tennessee initiated and led the petition.[11] "The latest news from the city of Washington states that there is probability of my appointment to the government of New Orleans," Jackson wrote Rachel from Knoxville.[12]

Jackson was so excited that he traveled to Washington to meet Thomas Jefferson and apply for the governorship. Once he got there, however, his republican principles triumphed over his self-interest. "Of all characters on earth," he explained to Congressman Campbell, "my feelings despise a man capable of cringing to power for a benefit of an office." He would not lobby for the position. "Under present circumstances my feelings could not consent to pay my respects to" President Jefferson, "least it might be construed into the conduct of a courteor." In a republic, "Meritt alone ought to be the road to preferment."[13] Ultimately, and not surprisingly given his scant regard for him, Jefferson decided against Jackson. Jackson found other ways, however, to serve his country and expand its borders.

The Indian Fighter

Jackson is famous, or notorious, for fighting and displacing Indians from the American frontier, but he actually held nuanced views about the Indians and was not the Indian hater of leftist myth. Much like Jefferson, Jackson believed the Indians were natural republicans with republican instincts and human rights guaranteed by God. But he believed the hard reality was that the Indians were well behind white Americans in terms of culture and civilization, a constant threat to the lives of settlers and their families, and a direct military threat likely to ally with America's European enemies. In a not atypical letter of his younger years, he wrote,

> The Late Express that [proclaimed peace] to our Western Country [attended with] the Late Depredations and [Murders] Committed by the Indians [on our] frontier has occassioned a Great [Claumour] amonghts the people of this [District] and it is Two Much to be [dreaded] that they Indians has made [use of] this Finesse to Lull the people to sleep that they might save [their Towns] and open a more Easy Road to [Commit] Murder with impunity; this [is proved] by their late conduct, for since [that] Express not Less than Twelve [have] been Killed and wounded in this [District]. One Question I would beg leave to [ask] why do we now attempt to hold a [Treaty—with them;] have they attended to the [Last] Treaty; I answer in the Negative [then] why do we attem[pt] to Treat with [a Savage] Tribe tha[t] will neither ad[here to] Treaties, nor the law of Nations, [upon these] particu[la]rs I would thank [you for] your Sent[i]ments."[14]

And a year later, he wrote something quite similar:

> I fear that their Peace Talks are only Delusions; and in order to put us off our Guard; why Treat with them.

Does not experience teach us that Treaties answer no other Purpose than opening an Easy door for the Indians to pass [through to] Butcher our Citizens; what [motives Congress are governed by with Respect to their] pacific Dispotison towards [them I] know not; some say humanity [dictates] it; but certainly she out [to Extend] and Equal share of humanity [to her own] Citizens; in doing this Congress [should act] Justly and Punish the Barbarians [for] Murdering her Innocent Citizens, has not our [Citizens] been Prosecuted for Marching to their [Town] and Killing some of them, [then why] not when they Commit Murders [on] our Citizens agreeable to Treaty [demand] the Egressors if they are not given [up]. It is an infringement of the Treaty [and a cause] of war and the whole [ought to be] Scurged for the infringement of [the Treaty] for as the Nation will not give [murderers] up when Demanded it is a Tacit [ack]knowledgement of their Consent to the [Com]mission of the Crime. Therefore all [con]senting are Equally guilty. I dread [the] Consequence of the Ensuing Sum[mer. The] Indians appear Verry Troublesome [on the] frontier. Discouraged and breaking and [num]bers leaving the Territory and moving [to] Kentuckey, this Country is Declining [fast] and unless Congress lends us a more am[ple] protection this Country will have at length [to break] or seek protection from some other Source than the present."[15]

Just as he considered himself a realist when it came to the Indians, and therefore a defender of harsh measures, Jackson also regarded himself as a realist when it came to whites, growing furious when they mistreated Indians and demanding that they be prosecuted and condemned.

Jackson had a very personal connection to the Indians—he had adopted an Indian boy as his son, an orphan brought to him during the War of 1812. Jackson loved the boy, Lyncoya, as his own and hoped to send him to West Point. With his growing religious faith, Jackson believed that Lyncoya might "have been given to me for some valuable purpose." Jackson wrote to Rachel that "When I reflect that he as to his relations is so much like myself [an orphan] I feel an unusual sympathy with him."[16]

The War of 1812, however, had also brought simmering tensions between whites and Indians to a boil. Shortly before the war, an Indian prophet—Tenskwatawa—called for a pan-Indian alliance to eradicate the whites. His brother, Tecumseh, put that into action, unifying the Indian tribes and allying them with the British.

Jackson offered to march his militia to aid General William Henry Harrison in Indiana after Tenskwatawa's and Tecumseh's forces fought Harrison's at the Battle of Tippecanoe on November 1, 1811.[17] But Jackson soon had trouble closer to home as the Creek Indians, encouraged by Tecumseh, chose to make war. Jackson wrote, "My heart bleeds within me at hearing of the wanton massacre of our women and children by a party of Creeks." Tecumseh was the "incendiary, the emissary of the Prophet, who is himself the tool of England," Jackson wrote to Tennessee's Governor Willie Blount.[18] Jackson's suspicion of a British-Indian alliance had come to reality—and to war.

The War of 1812

In 1811, Andrew Jackson's friend and ally, Representative Felix Grundy of Tennessee, delivered a speech in the House of Representatives to warn Congress of impending war:

> It cannot be believed by any man who will reflect, that the savage tribes, uninfluenced by other Powers, would think of making war on the United States. They understand too well their own weakness, and our strength. They have already felt the weight of our arms; they know they hold the very soil on which they live as tenants at sufferance. How, then, sir, are we to account for their late conduct? In one way only; some powerful nation must have intrigued with them, and turned their peaceful disposition towards us into hostilities. Great Britain alone has intercourse with those Northern tribes; I therefore infer, that if British gold has not been employed, their baubles and trinkets, and the promise of support and a place of refuge if necessary, have had their effect.... This war, if carried on successfully, will have its advantages. We shall drive the British from our Continent–they will no longer have an opportunity of

intriguing with out Indian neighbors, and setting on the ruthless savage to tomahawk our women and children. That nation will lose her Canadian trade, and, by having no resting place in this country, her means of annoying us will be diminished.... I am willing to receive the Canadians as adopted brethren: it will have beneficial political effects; it will preserve the equilibrium of the Government. When Louisiana shall be fully peopled, the Northern States will lose their power; they will be at the discretion of others; they can be pressured at pleasure, and then this Union might be endangered–I therefore feel anxious not only to add the Floridas to the South, but the Canadas to the North of this empire.[19]

On June 17, 1812, Jackson reported that his militia—made up of roughly 2,500 volunteers—was ready to move against the Creek Indians at the discretion of the governor. The next day, Congress declared war on Great Britain, and Governor Blount offered the services of Jackson, major general of the Tennessee militia, to the United States.[20] When no orders from Washington were forthcoming, Blount, on November 11, 1812, ordered Jackson and his men to New Orleans.[21] Marching through harsh winter weather, Jackson's army reached Natchez where it was ordered to halt and wait for further orders. Those orders didn't arrive until March 15 when the United States secretary of war ordered Jackson to disband his militia, return to Tennessee, and transfer such supplies as he had to General James Wilkinson, commander of U.S. Army forces in the area. Jackson adamantly refused the orders, noting that he would never abandon his men in hostile Indian country.[22] Instead, Jackson bore every financial burden and personally led the men back, noting that he had promised their mothers, sisters, and daughters that he would look out for them, no matter the cost. To his beloved wife, he explained his actions: "Their patriotism has been but illy rewarded by an ungrateful officer (not country) and it is therefore my duty to act as a father to the sick and to the well and stay with them until I march them into Nashville."[23]

Jackson "yielded up his horses to the sick, and trudging on foot, encountered all the hardships that were met by the soldiers."[24] John Reid (who witnessed these events) and John Eaton claimed that Jackson's troops not only respected and admired him but also came to love him as a father.[25] He was tough, one soldier said. As tough as hickory, another added. Soon, they called him "Hickory" and then "Old Hickory."[26]

It was after his ironically triumphant return to Nashville that Jackson saw action of a different kind—his bloody fight with Thomas and Jesse Benton that left him wounded and with a bullet permanently embedded in his shoulder. While recovering, he received news that a group of Creek Indians had brutally slaughtered civilians (even cutting babies out of pregnant women) on August 30, 1813, at Fort Mims, in current-day Alabama.[27] The southern frontiersmen were outraged, and Jackson, though still recovering, felt duty-bound to fight the Creeks. On October 7, 1813, Jackson led his militia against the Creeks, beginning a campaign that did not end until the decisive Battle of Horseshoe Bend on March 27, 1814. Jackson, in his official report, credited his subordinate officers and his Indian allies under Major William McIntosh: "The history of warfare I think furnishes few instances of a more brilliant attack." In addition to wiping out the hostiles, Jackson took 250 captives, "all women and children, except two or three."[28] Chief William Weatherford, leader of the hostile Creeks, surrendered to Jackson a few days later. Jackson pardoned the chief, and they became friends.[29] With Weatherford's surrender, Jackson officially declared the Creek campaign over.[30]

The campaign proved far more difficult for Jackson than the earlier 1812–1813 bureaucratic fiasco during which his troops named him "Old Hickory" for his fatherliness. On the Creek campaign, his men experienced many of the same privations as they had before—especially with the lack of food and shelter—but, this time, they rebelled against Jackson's orders, considering their own enlistments as nothing but voluntary.[31] Jackson was, understandably, confused and furious by these reactions. "I am sorry to say that my volunteer infantry, in whom I had so much confidence, and in whom our country had so much and who had acquired a Charictor for themselves and a reputation for their country are about to disgrace themselves by a mutinous disposition in the face of an enemy," Jackson wrote to Rachel.[32] He accepted all of the pains and sufferings of his men as his own, and, when in battle, he always fought with them at the very front, never hiding behind the lines. Though his duels were of his own choice, his body was suffering immensely from those decisions. "I have got to wearing my coat sleeve, and I hope ere long I will regain the use of my left arm," he confessed to Rachel, exactly six months after his duel with the Bentons. Constant fatigue plagued him as well.[33] His poor health showed visibly. When he arrived in New Orleans in December, one resident wrote of him, "His complexion was sallow and unhealthy, his hair iron grey, and his body thin and emaciated."[34] Regardless, he had seen this campaign against the Creeks not only as honorable but also as a way to build a road through the Mississippi Territory and take Florida from the Spanish. The former was necessary for settlement of the region while the latter was necessary to secure the gulf against any European invasion. Why could his men not also see these things? In his view, these resistors brought disgrace upon themselves and upon the very reputation of a republic, especially the American Republic.[35]

Still, the victory at the Battle of Horseshoe Bend proved critical to the defense of the gulf against the British as well as the Spanish. Should the British attempt a naval/marine operation against any of the southwestern states, they would not be able to rely upon native allies as their troops in the Great Lakes had done.

Though some of Jackson's militia had come to hate him, even more loved him. As did the United States, especially citizens living on the western frontier. Jackson had already been well known, but after his victory over the Creeks, he became such a popular figure that President Madison had to acknowledge it. Madison named Jackson a major general in the United States Army, finally giving him the recognition he so deserved and, as a republican and citizen soldier, had earned.[36] As always, Jackson knew he had to accept the position, but he did so with regret, realizing that this would take him farther from his beloved Rachel and The Hermitage. "It was with reluctance I accepted the office I now hold, had I thought was to have separated us again for length of time I certainly would have been at the Hermitage," he explained to Rachel. "But I have accepted, my honor never shall be stained—when danger rears its head, I can never shrink from it." It was not just honor for the republic, though. It was honor toward his mother and brothers and vengeance against empire. "I trust in a kind providence, for protection and success—I owe to Britain a debt of retaliatory vengeance. Should our forces meet I trust I shall pay the debt."[37]

The Battle of New Orleans

If the Creek campaign had made Jackson a household name across the United States, his actions at New Orleans made him nothing less than a republican demigod, a mythic figure equal to, at least in war, George Washington. Jackson performed brilliantly, despite being outrageously outnumbered and outgunned. Certainly, as he told Rachel, a republican will drove him and his actions against the British invaders.

The war against Napoleon had ended, and the British had defeated the French nobly and honorably. The North American theater of the Napoleonic Wars—at least from the English perspective—remained an obstinacy and a thorn. With the majority of their most honored diplomats meeting at the Congress of Vienna, the British sent their second and third-rate diplomats to treat with John Quincy Adams and Henry Clay. In December 1814, Adams and Clay reached an agreement with their British counterparts: *status quo ante bellum*. That is, everything would be as it was prior to the war. It would be, in some strange way, as if the war had never happened. Though the British were about to invade America again and the Americans knew peace talks were going on, neither side knew about the agreement until after the Battle of New Orleans. The British hoped that a third invasion of the United States (after the Great Lakes in 1812 and Washington and Baltimore in 1814) would give the British diplomats greater leverage in negotiating a peace. They could not have been more wrong.

Andrew Jackson, of course, had no way of knowing exactly where the British expeditionary force would land, but he knew that they would—at Mobile, Natchez, or New Orleans.[38] In the old Northwest, in 1812 and 1813, the British and their Indian allies had taken Fort Dearborn (Chicago) and Detroit. At Dearborn, they had massacred soldiers as well as women and children. They had almost taken Fort Wayne as well. In Washington, D.C., they had burned down the city. Their tactics, therefore, were obvious to Jackson. They would invade and destroy what they could, using their Indian allies to massacre innocents. By defeating the Creeks, however, Jackson had already denied them native allies outside of Spanish Florida. He had also attacked seven British ships near Pensacola on November 7, 1814, to demonstrate to the Spanish citizens there and to the British that they should not challenge the United States. Jackson included a regiment of Choctaw Indians to show that not all Indians were enemies of the United States. "The steady firmness of my troops has drawn a just respect from our enemies," he wrote to Governor Blount. The attack "has convinced the Spaniards of our friendship, and our prowess, and has drawn from the citizens an expression, that our Choctaws are more civilized than the British."[39] Knowing Jackson's reputation, but not having known him, many in Pensacola feared Jackson as a pillager and plunderer before he arrived in town. Instead, "Genl. J. and his army have obtained for themselves a lasting name for their humanity and good order," one witness recorded. "Not a single excess was committed," and the town's view of Jackson went quickly from fear to admiration.[40]

Again, not knowing precisely where the British would invade, Jackson fortified the various water inlets of the gulf as best he could. In late December, he realized the invasion would take place at New Orleans, and he ordered himself and his men transportation there as quickly as possible. While in transit to New Orleans, his boat, the *Carolina*, encountered British troops on December 23—resulting in a two-hour battle with them—before he could proceed to New Orleans. As Jackson began his fortification of the city, the British engaged him in a brief artillery exchange on January 1. The American forces claimed victory. As part of his fortifications, Jackson persuaded and recruited a justly (in)famous group of men to stave off the British. With him, he had his own Tennesseans, Kentuckians under John Adair, Louisiana militia, and several, free, (Franco-American) black regiments. Perhaps most infamously, he also recruited some local pirates to fight with him as well. In so many ways, Jackson's variegated army was the very best of America, writ small. Because he had, relatively speaking, so few men and since most of them were volunteer militia, Jackson immediately decided upon a defensive position.[41]

The British forces, consisting of roughly sixty naval ships and 14,000 troops, led by the inept General Edward Pakenham, launched a full-scale invasion of American soil on January 8, 1815. Explaining why the English aristocratic selection of officers had become dangers to the empire itself, Paul Johnson, British historian and journalist, writes,

> The great Duke of Wellington [Pakenham] had married his sister, Catherine, but that was the closest he got to military mastery. Money and connections had made him a major before he was 17 and a colonel at 21. There was no question of his courage. Serving as major-general under his brother-in-law at Salamanca in 1812, he had been given his chance when Wellington told him

to take his division straight at the French center, with the words "Now's your time, Ned!" He broke through the French line and this, said Wellington in his dispatch, won the battle, though he admitted "Pakenham may not be the brightest genius."[42]

Jackson had so perfectly entrenched, fortified, and positioned his 2,000 men that any British landing was met with brilliant and brutal crossfire—American sharpshooters leveled the British invaders, one by one, rank by rank. Relatively soon after the invasion had begun, Jackson's 2,000 men had cut down over 2,000 British marines, including their commander, Pakenham. Jackson estimated that he and his militia had killed nearly 1,500 British marines and had captured at least 500 prisoners. "My loss has not exceeded and I believe has not amounted to ten killed and as many wounded," Jackson reported. [43] Stunned, British General John Lambert called for a ceasefire. Greatly outnumbered and fearful of the British knowing it, Jackson agreed. Though the two sides still occasionally exchanged fire over the next eleven days, the British forces departed for home on January 19. Jackson reported that the British would most likely not return and that "Louisiana is now clear of the enemy."[44]

Indeed, the British had just experienced one of the most bitter defeats in their history, and it certainly colored their view of British victories in the Napoleonic Wars. However, as Paul Johnson explains, it was this defeat that made the British, finally, respect and even befriend America—no longer an upstart republic—as a power to be feared and admired. The two nations would antagonize each other over the next century, but they came to realize that what they shared in language, culture, law, and manners made them more unified than divided.[45]

Jackson was now as great as his heroes, William Wallace and James Wolfe. Against all odds, he had created a republican army out of a group of militias, undisciplined rogues, and anyone else able and willing to bear arms alongside him. In a public ceremony of honor, the Reverend William Dubourg told Jackson that the city of New Orleans was now "the true bulwark of independence, is now re-echoing from shore to shore your splendid achievements and preparing to inscribe your name on her immortal rolls among those of her Washingtons." To which Jackson graciously responded, "That is has been effected with so little loss, that so few tears should cloud the smiles of our triumph, and not a cypress leaf be interwoven in the wreath which you present, is a source of the most exquisite enjoyment."[46] He was no longer Major General Andrew Jackson or even Old Hickory; he was both these things and more. Jackson was "The Hero of New Orleans" and the man who finally taught the British that America was here to stay. After the Battle of New Orleans, neither nation could deny that Americans were not British subjects; they were their equals. Perhaps even their superiors.

Chapter Four

Conqueror and Hero

After the Battle of New Orleans, Jackson's fame spread from America to Europe where he was known as the "Napoleon of the Woods," at once a demigod and a living myth.[1] As with Napoleon, politicians feared him. President James Madison (1809–1817) and President James Monroe (1817–1825) felt they needed him because of his immense popularity and military skill, but they were also afraid of him because Jackson seemed all too likely to overstep his authority and instructions. And, to be fair to Madison and Monroe, it remains unclear by what authority Jackson made his most important decisions between 1814 and 1821. At the beginning of the War of 1812,

Jackson had been the head of the Tennessee militia, a major general. By 1814, he was a major general in the United States Army. During his campaign against the Seminoles, 1816–1819, he often acted as a member of the U.S. Army and, equally often when it suited him, as head of the Tennessee militia. The lines that separated volunteer militia from the federal army were not so clear then, and Jackson was simply America's premier general.

Pensacola

Jackson had long believed that Spanish Florida represented a grave threat to the integrity of the American republic. Not only did it provide a gateway for hostile powers to invade the United States through the Gulf of Mexico, but the Spaniards were either unable or unwilling to prevent Indians and runaway slaves from using Spanish Florida as a base from which to raid Americans who lived in southern Georgia.

On April 23, 1816, General Jackson informed the Spanish authorities that if they did nothing to stop Indians and blacks from attacking Americans, he would be forced to invade Spanish territory and demolish the Negro Fort, the rebels' headquarters.[2] Mauricio de Zuniga, the Spanish governor of West Florida, responded more than a month later, saying that the fort was not countenanced by Spain, that it should indeed be destroyed, and suggested that British agents might be working mischief there. But he asked Jackson not to invade Spanish territory even if the threat from the Negro Fort continued.[3] Ignoring the Spanish governor, Jackson attacked and destroyed the Negro Fort on July 27, 1816. A month later, with diplomatic relations frayed, three Spanish ships attacked and captured an American vessel, the USS *Firebrand*.

—

When James Monroe was sworn in as president in 1817, Jackson was thrilled. Monroe, he believed, was a true statesman, and, with the country in good hands, Jackson considered retirement.[4] But President Monroe begged him not to. "I need not state that it is my earnest desire that you remain in the service of your country." Given the threat posed by Spain and the revolutionary sentiments taking hold of their Latin American colonies, the country might have need of him. "Our affairs are not settled, and nothing is more uncertain than the time," he told Jackson.[5] Jackson promised the president he would remain in the United States Army at least until the spring of 1818.[6]

Meanwhile, the Indian and black raiders of Spanish Florida continued to threaten the citizens of Georgia. In response, Secretary of War John C. Calhoun instructed Jackson to take action using both militia and federal troops. "With this view you may be prepared to concentrate your forces and to adopt the necessary measures to terminate a conflict which it has ever been the desire of the President, from considerations of humanity, to avoid; but which is now made necessary by their Settled hostilities," Calhoun ordered.[7] Jackson was essentially given *carte blanche* to do what he deemed necessary. Jackson trusted his Tennessee militia and assumed that federal assistance would be largely imaginary.[8] In a telling letter to Secretary of War Calhoun, he stated that should the federal government find itself unable to create arsenals and foundries for the defense of the republic, Jackson would find private citizens who were more than willing to pay the cost. Jackson reminded Calhoun that such private provision of goods would keep the region independent of foreign *or domestic* powers that did not have their best interests in mind.[9]

Jackson invaded Florida, promising to respect the rights and property of innocent Spaniards but offering no mercy for raiders or anti-American forces. He burned towns, took hostages, and seized strategic points.[10] Convinced that European agents were using the Seminoles and blacks as pawns against the United States, Jackson captured two British citizens in Florida, Alexander Arbuthnot and Robert C. Ambrister. The Britons were tried, found guilty, and executed by a "Special Court of Select Officers." Jackson fully supported the court's decision. He also informed the secretary of war that he intended to garrison several captured towns and seize Pensacola.[11] Having invaded Florida, he saw no reason to leave it, and nineteen days later, on May 24, 1818, Jackson's forces occupied Pensacola.[12] Jackson said diplomats could work out the details but informed the Spanish authorities that he was there by right of self-defense.[13] Jackson wrote his wife, "I have destroyed the babylon of the South, the hotbed of the Indian war & depredations on our frontier, by taking St. Marks

& Pensacola." Throughout the campaign, he assured Rachel that God's hand had guided the Americans.[14]

When President Monroe and his administration realized that Jackson had virtually annexed West Florida, they were stunned. Monroe shot off a letter to Jackson, informing him that he had exceeded his orders and his authority and had unwisely threatened war with Spain.[15] Certainly, Jackson's actions had thrown Monroe's cabinet into disarray. So upset was Monroe by the news, that he unwisely left Washington for vacation on June 26, a week after receiving the news, and did not return until July 14. During that time, Secretary of State John Quincy Adams repeatedly listened to the anger and concerns expressed by the British, French, and Spanish ambassadors. Adams considered the position he would ultimately take on Jackson's actions in Florida as reflecting his own integrity and republicanism. "Above all, that, till I die, I may not suffer my integrity to depart from me, and that whatever dispensation of Providence hereafter awaits me, I may be prepared to receive it with prudence, temperance, justice, and fortitude," he confided in his diary. He thought his decision and his support or rejection of Jackson in this matter was not just one of a series of decisions in his life, but a profoundly critical one for his soul. When Monroe finally returned from his ill-timed vacation, he called the cabinet together. The cabinet discussed nothing but Jackson from June 15 until June 20. John Quincy Adams decided in every matter that Jackson had been correct, and he served as the lone voice in support of him. He thought Jackson had upheld

the "law of nations" as well as the U.S. Constitution in his defense
of American rights against Spanish and Indian depredations.
Jackson's main opponent in the cabinet was John C. Calhoun who
seemed "personally offended" by Jackson's actions. Finally, on
July 21, John Quincy Adams, without changing his mind, conceded that he had lost the debate with the cabinet. Still, he worried
the cabinet's decision was unjust and weak.[16]

Whatever the Monroe administration claimed, however,
Jackson would not back down. He had been given *carte blanche*
to do what was necessary, and he had done it. If Spain was embar-
rassed, it was her own fault for being incompetent. The failing
empire claimed authority but had neither the ability nor the desire
to use it, thus endangering the lives and rights of law-abiding
citizens. Additionally, he claimed, his actions in Florida had demonstrated to Europe's growing Holy Alliance that its members
should not interfere with the United States.[17]

For nearly a year, the debate raged over whether Jackson's
actions were justified. Secretary of State John Quincy Adams
remained his sole supporter. In Congress, Henry Clay led the
charge against Jackson, and Jackson never forgave him for it. One
of Jackson's closest allies, Governor Willie Blount of Tennessee,
called Clay and his allies "poor minded bitches."[18] On February
8, 1819, Congress handily voted down four resolutions condemn-
ing Jackson. Adams used Congress's support of Jackson—and the
threat of Jackson's unpredictable nature—to convince Spain to
sell Florida to the United States and officially approve the borders

of the Louisiana Purchase.[19] To the American people, Jackson had not only been right, he had been magnificent; he seemed the embodiment of the American spirit.

Governor of Florida

To capitalize on Jackson's popularity, Monroe visited him at The Hermitage on June 5, 1819. For days, Nashville celebrated the two men. From June 14 until July 11, they toured Kentucky together. Though Monroe still had reservations about Jackson, he was keen to keep him on his side.[20]

Jackson supported Monroe in the 1820 presidential election but had reservations of his own. Monroe tried to assuage him by naming Jackson the territorial governor of Florida on March 10, 1821.[21] Jackson accepted but on the condition that he could retire after his establishment of an effective government.[22] Jackson wrote to one of his nephews, "I sincerely regret that I did not adhere to my first determination not to accept the Government of Floridas (East and West Florida), your aunt appears very reluctant to go to that climate and really I am wearied with public life."[23] "When I return," he wrote to his close friend, John Coffee, "I return permanently as a [private] citizen."[24]

As governor, Jackson was baffled by many Spanish customs but maintained Spanish civil and property law to defend the existing rights of Spanish settlers. He also extended English common law into Florida, especially in criminal matters.[25] "I have kept steadily in view the securing to the inhabitants of the Floridas all the privileges and immunities guaranteed to them by the treaty [transferring sovereignty to the United States]," Jackson announced officially. "The principal of these is the protection of their persons, property, and religion, until they shall be incorporated into the Union, and become entitled to all the privileges and immunities of citizens of the United States."[26] He also extended the right to vote to all men, regardless of race, religion, ethnicity, or property ownership. "The American government, at the same time that it is the freest, is perhaps the strongest in the world; because the wealthiest and most powerful in society are as weak in opposition to it, as the most humble and obscure," Jackson reasoned. "It knows no distinction between an ex-governor and a peasant." [27] He explained his policies to a military colleague; his explanation suggests a belief in radical democracy:

> Under existing circumstances, it would be impolitic & unjust to make a property qualification. Residence alone, in justice to all, should be required. This is the only republican rule that can be established, untill your land titles are adjudicated, and your vacant and apropriated land brought into markett—and you come into the union as a state. Then in your constitution you can adopt such qualifications as you may think proper for the happiness, security, & prosperity of the state. Untill then all freemen of six months residence should be entitled to vote. All freeman residents will be bound by

your laws, & subject to punishment under them—and
of right, ought to be entitled to a voice in making
them.[28]

In the spring of 1821, Jackson was forced to resign his army
commission, as the federal government was reducing the army
(something that even Jackson, the great defender of the militia,
thought was shortsighted). He resigned as governor of Florida on
November 13, 1821, having pronounced, two months earlier, that
the government was now fully established.[29] Congress and the
president received the notice on December 4, 1821.[30]

The Republic and Wyoming

But whatever thoughts Jackson had about retirement, he was
not done serving his country. On July 26, 1822, Tennessee's legislature nominated him for the presidency of the United States. In
Jackson, the legislature resolved, "they behold the soldier, the
statesman, and the honest man; he deliberates, he decides, and he
acts; he is calm in deliberation, cautious in decision, efficient in
action. Such a man we are willing to aid in electing to the highest
office in the gift of a free people."[31]

Part of what propelled enthusiasm for Jackson's candidacy
was a feeling that the country needed a revival of its old republican spirit. Historian Gordon Wood claimed that "all the major
revolutionary leaders died less than happy with the results of the
Revolution."[32] Mercy Otis Warren, a gifted female supporter of

the American Revolution and an anti-Federalist, published her three-volume history of the Revolution in 1805. It struck a similar disappointed chord. Liberty, she noted, now meant little more than avarice. "Though the name of liberty delights the ear," she wrote, "and tickles the fond pride of man," mammon had replaced morality and patriotism. America, she lamented, "has in great measure lost her simplicity of manners...; the Americans are already in too many instances hankering after the sudden accumulation of wealth, and the proud distinctions of fortune and title. They have too far lost that general sense of moral obligation, formerly felt by all classes in America."[33]

In 1823, writing under the pen name "Wyoming," Senator John Henry Eaton of Tennessee—a longtime admirer of Jackson's and coauthor of *The Life of Jackson*, published in 1817—made the case that Jackson was the man who could restore America's republican virtue.[34] As with many of the pamphlets of the revolutionary era, *The Letters of Wyoming* are uneven in style and argumentation. When they are good, they are very good. When they are bad—generally when attacking a political opponent of Andrew Jackson—they are embarrassingly bad.

From the opening pages of his pamphlet series, Wyoming attacks the city of Washington as a center of corruption "springing into existence, and fast flourishing."[35] In that hell, "Intrigue passes for talent and corruption has usurped the place of virtue." The people, for whom the city should be dedicated, have lost their place as the "wakeful guardians of their country's rights." As with so many previous generations, they assumed their liberty was permanent, and they slumbered. In the eighth letter, Wyoming lays it out directly:

> Our country has been gradually receding from first principles since that period, when the father of his country yielded up the almost shattered bark, which he had borne in safety through the storms of the Revolution. The places and posts which then were occupied by reason, prudence, and love of country, are now found in the possession of intrigue, management, and corruption.[36]

With this paragraph, Wyoming at once sounds like Mercy Otis Warren as well as the ancient republicans Cicero and Livy.

In what was certainly the beginning of the long American tradition of "it will take an outsider to fix Washington," Wyoming noted repeatedly that General Jackson had no ties to the city, no connection with any party or faction, and no obligations or debts to any member of the federal government. He had, however, served the republic repeatedly as a natural leader and a defender. "Jackson stands alone, the 'People's Candidate.'"[37] He had done so, the author pointed out, during the American Revolution, in the wars against the Indians, and when he successfully repelled a British invasion of the gulf coast. Never had Jackson done this for self-interested reasons, only for the good of the republic. Wyoming noted a speech Jackson gave in 1815, during his defense of New Orleans:

> Your government, Louisianians, is engaged in a just and honourable contest, for the security of your individual, and her national rights. The only country on earth where man enjoys freedom; where its blessings are alike extended to the poor and to the rich, calls on you to protect her from the grasping usurpation of Britain:—she will not call in vain. I know that every man whose bosom beats high at the proud title of freeman, will promptly obey her voice, and rally round the eagles of his country, resolved to rescue her, from impending danger, or nobly die in her defence. Who refuses to defend his rights when called on by his government, deserves to be a slave—deserves to be punished as an enemy to his country—a friend to her foes.[38]

In his third letter, Wyoming asks his most difficult question. Is the federal government working as the founding fathers intended? Wyoming argues that the legislative branch had overstepped its boundaries, become a tool of party chieftains, and was usurping executive and judicial power.

Wyoming warned that members of the House and, especially, the Senate were positioning themselves to become America's new and permanent aristocrats. "For an Aristocracy is rising in our land, and soon, very soon, the people of this country, with all their boasted privileges, will become the mere instruments of the men in power."[39] They would not call themselves an aristocracy for the people would immediately understand what and who they were. Instead, they would go under the false name of the "leading men of the country." They seek nothing, however, but to make the people serve in "miserable dependence."[40] It would be best, Wyoming contended, if the aristocrats proclaimed themselves as such.

> If we are to be controlled by a *privileged order,* for heaven's sake let us know it; and let stars and garters decorate their royal personages, that we may know them; it will be far better than to have a parcel of sanctified pretenders stalking through the country in sheep's clothing, preaching up and proclaiming their republican principles, and feelings, and purity, while at the same time they are seeking to obtain consequence, and to elevate themselves by secretly attempting to undermine the checks and balances of the government.[41]

Ignorance should not excuse a republican people from guilt. "Let the people look to this, and remember, they deserve to be, what ere they will be, slaves, if they suffer themselves to be cajoled out of their rights reserved to them by the constitution."[42]

"It is true that a tyranny which is best concealed is most tolerable," he admits, "yet it does not on that account cease to be tyranny."[43] The demagogues flatter and cajole in the name of "the people," but in the end they, and the bureaucrats that serve them—those who "hang on[to] office, sucking in the sustenance of the country"[44]—work ceaselessly to undermine the republic.

No country ever lost at once, its privileges and its rights: generally, the principles of all free and liberal Governments have been sapped, not by sudden, but, by slow and imperceptible marches. It has ever been a part of the attribute of power, to strain the cord a little, and a little closer, until like piling mites in a scale, the senses are conscious of the addition only when the balance begins to veer. England, next to our own, perhaps, the freest government, has repeatedly beheld her kings making inroads beyond the sanction of regal prerogative, and not unfrequently have they been reined in by the people; not when the evils were at their commencement, but when the nation awakened from its reverie, and beheld there was a departure from first principles.[45]

These "leading men" and their bureaucrats have created a kind of European court that exists for "flattery, folly, and intrigues," thus undermining the simple virtues of an agrarian and republican people.[46] Such corruption fed on the cities.

I am indeed sorry to see mv country manifest such fondness and partiality for exotics. In manners, dress, and language, we are imitators, and borrowers from a road; native genius sinks in comparison, with that which is foreign, and even our appetites mark the inferior flavour of our own, when contrasted with the products of a foreign soil. All that we have national, is our government, and even that, ere long, without much caution, will have introduced into it, many notions and idioms, other than the growth of this country; already have some appeared: witness for example those things called etiquette and courtly parade (and nonsense) so much in vogue at our metropolis. I want a man, my countrymen, at the head of this nation, who will throw such trifles off; one who shall give us to see something of republican plainness, and who may have character enough to induce a belief that it is right.[47]

God and nature ask no person to "arrogate to himself, the right of determining for others what things are proper, and what not."[48] The "leading men" put on the appearances of wisdom and pretend that through their leadership they will perfect America. This is a "delusion" at every level, as perfection can never exist in this world. Nature—its good and its bad—does not change by people or time or place. It remains consistent through all times and all places and all peoples. "In Republican America, the same thirst for domination exists, as is to be found in the despotic nation as of Europe."[49] Skilled at deception, the "leading men of the day" have created Washington as a sort of theater upon which they hang "beautiful decorations," but, in reality, these are superficial, "a mere phantasmagoria, representing and exhibiting as real, things that are altogether illusory."[50] They have, through their zeal, turned Washington into a new Mecca, a shrine for the political pilgrim to gain gilded milk from the gilded calf.[51]

The founding fathers understood all these dangers well and did what they could to prevent them from developing. To that end, the American people must be reminded that the three branches of government should be in tension, not harmony,[52] and that "Without virtue, liberty cannot exist—they are handmaids and sisters that dwell together, and that will not, cannot, be separated."[53]

The first four letters of Wyoming are, at their best, timeless. The middle letters deal with the character of Andrew Jackson, and the final letters bash Jackson's opponents. Wyoming argues that Jackson will reanimate the republic because he embodies America's republican virtues.[54] He compares Jackson to noble Cincinnatus of Rome, who would rather live in stoic solitude on his farm, never seeking office, but also would never ignore his duty when called upon. "Jackson is the only man before the nation, who, resting in the shade of private life, is without patronage or favour, by which to win to him partisans and friends."[55]

Moreover, he had fought for the republic, leading free men into battle against the Seminoles, the Creeks, the Spanish, and the British. His "efficiency of conduct, his boldness of character, and fearless intrepidity, whenever his country called upon him for his services" make him a republican hero and the most feared enemy of the demagogues.[56]

> Let the nation answer then, where amongst them is there a republican like ANDREW JACKSON? Does he love his country? Let a head grown grey, a constitution impaired in the service of that country, declare! Let our protected borders, saved from Indian barbarity, and the slaughtered thousands of Europe's chosen veterans, on the plains of New Orleans, proclaim.[57]

Jackson was the man who could save the republic from its enemies, foreign and domestic. In particular, Wyoming claims, Americans must be wary of the European Holy Alliance of Prussia, Russia, and Austria, self-proclaimed guardians of monarchical privileges against republican longings. Should they turn their eyes toward the Americas, they would hesitate when they saw the Hero of New Orleans protecting this hemisphere.[58]

Chapter Five

The Reluctant President

There is no evidence that Jackson had any presidential ambitions before 1821. In fact, his primary objective after serving as governor of Florida was pursuing a quiet retirement at The Hermitage.

But others had different ideas. On August 1, 1821, Samuel Ragland Overton, who had just returned from Philadelphia, informed Jackson that "the dominant party in Pennsylvania are determined to run you as a candidate for the next Presidency."[1] What Jackson thought of this is, unfortunately, lost to history, but most likely he was unenthused. Neither Jackson nor his wife were eager to leave Nashville or hobnob with the ruling Eastern elite. Moreover, Jackson knew that Secretary of State John Quincy Adams, a man he respected, was positioned to be elected president. Thomas Jefferson, James Madison, and James Monroe had each served as secretary of state and used that position as a training ground for the presidency; it seemed likely that Adams would do the same. "You know my private opinion of Mr. Adams," Jackson wrote to James Gadsden in December 1821, his "talents, virtue, and integrity." He added, "I think him a man of the first rate mind of any in america as a civilian and scholar—and I never doubted of his attachment to our republican Government."[2] A month later, even after the Nashville papers began to tout Jackson as a candidate, Jackson said the American people should elect either John Quincy Adams or John C. Calhoun to the White House in 1824 because both men would ensure that American "rights liberties & properties may be long protected, and our republican government in its purity agreeable to our constitution may be perpetuated."[3] Six month later, however, at the end of June 1822, Jackson acquiesced—at least slightly—to the clamor for a presidential run. "The voice of the people I am told would bring me to the Presidential chair, and it is probable, some of the Legislatures may bring my name before the Public," Jackson grudgingly admitted to a friend. "I have long since determined to be perfectly Silent—I never have been a candidate for office, I never will." But he conceded, "The people have a right to call for any mans service in a republican government—and when they do, it is the duty of the individual, to yield his services to that call."[4] When the legislature of Tennessee nominated Jackson for the presidency on July 27 (House) and August 3 (Senate), Jackson quietly accepted. He refused, however, to campaign for the office. He gave no speeches; he made no vote-gathering tours.

The following year, 1823, the Tennessee state legislature elected him to the United States Senate.[5] Dutifully, between 1823 and 1825, Senator Andrew Jackson participated in national debates in Washington, but, as before, he never relished the position. Rachel did not like Washington either. "Mrs. J is more disconsolate than I ever knew her before, and I do assure you I leave home with more reluctance than I ever did in my life, it was so unlooked for, unwished for and so inconsistent with my feeling," he admitted to John Overton.[6] The crowds that amassed to greet him en route to Washington stunned him;[7] they helped him realize that he was indeed a national political figure.

As before, he did not like the life of a legislator. As noted in previous chapters, though he was intelligent and witty, Jackson was a doer rather than a thinker. He had given long and hard thought to military matters, family, friendship, law, republics, and Christianity, but he was always most comfortable living by a few, well-crafted Stoic and republican maxims than by an overactive mind. As soon as he could—immediately after losing the presidential election of 1824 to John Quincy Adams— Jackson resigned his Senate seat, happy to return to his home state and The Hermitage. As Robert Remini has convincingly argued, this short term in the Senate proved critical to Jackson's ultimate acceptance in Washington. During this term, he kept his temper, mended fences with men such as Thomas Hart Benton, and forged new alliances. For the Washington scene, he had proven himself a capable and steady man, not merely the wild frontiersman of myth. He appeared civil, armed with frontier weapons of retribution.[8] A tribute to that fact was that his 1824 campaign for president had won the support of Charles Carroll of Carrollton, one of the Maryland signers of the Declaration of Independence.

The 1824 campaign was a hard-fought affair, and Jackson's opponents used his military background to label him a new "Julius Caesar," ready to take down the republic in the name of despotic efficiency. "The friends of Roman liberty warned the people of the danger of trusting their government in the hands of an ambitious military man, telling them that he would subvert their liberties, and which he accordingly did," an Ohioan wrote. "The friends of American liberty are now warning and admonishing the people of the United States of the danger of placing an ambitious military man at the head of the government, and as a proof of the danger are pointing them to the fate of the Roman republic, which was overthrown by her great 'military chieftain.'"[9]

"Military chieftain" appeared everywhere—in papers and speeches in both the 1824 and 1828 presidential campaigns—with the implication that having a "military chieftain" as president would destroy the republic. On the very eve of the 1828 election, one paper wrote,

Some persons allege that because Gen. Jackson fought well for his country, he must be honest and faithful, and make a good president. But Benedict Arnold fought bravely for his country, and yet became a traitor. Aaron Burr fought well, but afterwards conspired against the Union of his country. Bolivar fought for Colombia, but is now destroying her liberty. Cromwell fought for liberty, but afterwards betrayed it. Wellington fought for England; but now opposes the interests and liberties of the English people. Napoleon fought for the liberty of France, but finally destroyed it. Ilurbide fought for Mexico, and afterwards made himself Emperor, and was shot as a Traitor. Morillo fought for Spain, but helped to destroy Spanish liberty. Sylla fought for Rome, but afterwards marched an army into the city and massacred the people. Marius, of Rome, followed the example of Sylla. Caesar followed in the same path. It is madness then to vote for a man merely because he fought with bravery and success. Even robbers and pirates do the same.[10]

Congressman Henry Clay of Kentucky popularized the term "military chieftain" as one of abuse against Jackson. As Speaker of the House of Representatives in 1824, he proved Jackson's most prominent and important critic. Clay said he could never support any man whose claim to fame rested solely on his military skills.[11]

To his credit, Jackson embraced the epithet as a compliment. "It is very true, that early in life, even in the days of my boyhood, I contributed my mite to shake off the yoke of tyranny, and to build up the fabric of free government," he explained. "When lately our country was involved in war, bearing then the commission of Major Genl of Militia in Tennessee, I made an appeal. To the patriotism of the western citizens, when 3000 of them went with me to the field, to support her Eagles."[12] If this meant that Jackson was a "military chieftain," then so be it. Besides, which was worse, the demagogue, backed by a standing army, or a military chieftain who calls up volunteers for a short time for the defense of hearth and home?[13]

Of course, it was exactly his military prowess that attracted many, if not most, American voters. Jackson was "the great preserver of the glorious fabric of our independence, raised by the immortal Washington, as the hero who saved our banners at New Orleans from the unhallowed touch of Gen. Packenham, at a time when the legislature of Louisiana were actually engaged in deliberating the question whether they should not surrender the capital and state to the British army," a Maryland committee proclaimed in early 1824.[14] Such sentiments were offered at every meeting at every level of the republic in favor of Jackson.

While Jackson won the popular vote in the 1824 election—easily beating Vice President John Quincy Adams, House Speaker Henry Clay, and Secretary of the Treasury William Crawford—the electoral college votes proved inconclusive. That Jackson had

won ninety-nine of the votes, Adams had won eighty-four, Crawford had won forty-one, and Clay had won thirty-seven meant
that no candidate had a plurality, and the contest was thrown to
the House of Representatives. Still a U.S. senator, Jackson refused
to speak publicly about the election prior to the final House vote,
taken on February 9, 1825. Quietly, Jackson longed to lose so that
he could go back to The Hermitage.[15] "How often does my
thoughts lead me back to the Hermitage there in private life surrounded with a few friends, would be a paradise, compared to
the best situation here," he confided to a friend.[16]

As Jackson stood by, stoically, Henry Clay maneuvered with
Machiavellian deftness to throw the House election to John
Quincy Adams. Representative Robert P. Letcher of Kentucky
visited Adams on December 17, 1824. "The drift of all of Letcher's discourse," Adams recorded in his diary, was "that Clay
would willingly support me if he could thereby serve himself,
and the substance of his meaning was, that if Clay's friends
could know that he would have a prominent share in the Administration, that might induce them to vote for me, even in the face
of instructions."[17] Though far subtler than Letcher, Clay met
with Adams directly on January 9, 1825. Clay believed it essential "to prepare and predispose all his friends to a state of neu-
trality between the three candidates"—Adams, Jackson, and
William Crawford—"so that they might be free ultimately to
take that course which might be most conducive to the public
interest."[18] Clay told Adams that the election of Andrew Jackson

would be "the greatest calamity which could befall the country." Clay said he supported Adams but in the end wanted only what was good for the country.[19] On January 21, 1825, Adams assured a group of Clay's friends that "if I should be elected by the suffrages of the West, I should naturally look to the West for much of the support that I should need."[20] Eight days later, on January 29, Clay and Adams talked long into the night, though Adams, atypically, offered no details of the conversation other than that "he spoke to me with the utmost freedom of men and things."[21] On February 9, the House met, electing John Quincy Adams as the sixth president of the United States. Each state received one vote in the process. Thirteen states, including Clay's Kentucky, voted for Adams, seven states voted for Jackson, and four states voted for Crawford. Three days later, on February 12, Adams offered the position of secretary of state to Henry Clay.[22]

Andrew Jackson and his friends referred to this as a "corrupt bargain," and Jackson asserted that Clay's men had offered him the same quid pro quo—Clay's support in exchange for high office. That Clay's men talked with Jackson is certain. That they dropped hints of political favors and exchanges is also certain. That Clay supported their efforts, however, while likely, is not certain. Given Jackson's temper and character, he would never have accepted such a trade with Clay, whom he despised. "Jackson you well know will not intrigue or trade for any thing in the shape of office, & I love the man, the more that he will not," Senator

Eaton wrote privately to Judge Overton.[23] Future President James Buchanan served as an intermediary between Clay and Jackson, and, as he lied whenever it was convenient for his own career, we will never know exactly what transpired.[24]

The British, to be sure, breathed a sigh of relief when they learned of Adams's election:

> We do not look with any great approbation on this part of Mr. Quincy Adams's political career, yet candour obliges us to say that we no where trace in his conduct the violence and bigotry of a blind hater of England. His writings, if not very profound, are moderate; his personal deportment is said to be mild and pleasant, and his mind is certainly to a certain degree cultivated. When we compare him with his competitor, General Jackson, the contrast is striking. Jackson has always been a Democrat; and as Democrats in power are generally despotic, his conduct as a General was arbitrary and ferocious in the extreme. He is the favorite of the mob; because the mob is always servile, and always ready to follow an armed and arbitrary leader. The mob of England were for Cromwell, the mob of Rome for Caesar, and the mob of France for Bonaparte.[25]

The entire spectacle of Washington politics disgusted Jackson. "How humiliating to the American charecter that its high functionaries should so conduct themselves, as to become liable to the imputation of bargain & sale of the constitutional rights of the people," he lamented.[26] "Mr Clay had influence anough to Barter the votes of Kenty Missouri, Elinoi, Louisiana," he wrote to John Overton. "Thus you see here, the voice of the people of the west have been disregarded and demagogues barter them as sheep in the shambles."[27]

To Jackson, Clay was the "Judas of the West," selling the republic for a mere "thirty pieces of silver."[28] Jackson's friends and supporters rallied behind him and made decrying the "corrupt bargain" their battle cry for the next four years. A correspondent from New York wrote to Jackson that "Jackson, greater in adversity than in prosperity, is the only man who can rally the nation & restore the Govt to its primitive purity."[29] These were words Jackson did not want to hear. But even before he and his wife returned home, the campaign for 1828 was underway. The Tennessee legislature formally nominated him for the presidency on October 6, 1825. Jackson's republican principles would not let him refuse. "The moment the Legislature of Tennessee again brought my name before the nation as a candidate for the presidency on the next canvass, political consistency at once point[ed me] to the course I must adopt."[30] In early March 1826, the legislature of Pennsylvania also nominated Jackson, and other states and localities soon followed.[31]

Three days after Jackson had arrived at The Hermitage in April, a group of militias escorted him into Nashville where speeches, festivities, and an artillery salute greeted him as a republican savior. Moved, but undoubtedly exhausted from his return trip and increasingly poor health, Jackson delivered a short but powerful speech. He stated that he had been with his fellow Nashvillians from the beginning, breaking the wilderness, resisting the American Indians, and cultivating civilization. "We clung together," he noted. Many of the original inhabitants "now sleep with their fathers," but their children have repeatedly responded to the call of patriotism, defending against Indian barbarism and European despotism. With nothing but "pity," the people of Tennessee had time and again undermined the supposed "invincibility of tyrants." Providence alone, Jackson assured the crowd, placed him among such excellent people, each a friend and republican. "The Presidential chair I have always viewed as a situation too responsible to be sought after, by any individual, however great his talents, or eminent his services," he stated sincerely. One must approach the position with "awful forbodings." As a republican, though, he would neither seek the office nor deny it. The fate of Jackson's future rested with the American people and God.[32]

Jackson never questioned the constitutionality of John Quincy Adams's presidency. But he did withdraw his previous support of Adams as a republican statesman, telling Henry Lee, Robert E. Lee's father, that republican morality "forbids an association with those whom we believe corrupt or capable of cherishing vice when it ministers to selfish aggrandizement."[33]

"The Party of Jackson"

Exactly when political parties formed in America remains a mystery. However, drawing upon the work of political historians—such as Arthur Schlesinger Jr.—modern historians have generally accepted that the Federalists and Anti-Federalists made up the first party system. The Anti-Federalists quickly became "Republicans," "Jeffersonians," or "Democratic-Republicans," a ridiculous moniker generally used in textbooks. No person in the 1790s or early 1800s called himself or herself a "Democratic-Republican." This is a purely anachronistic term, first thrust upon the past in the 1830s. While many, especially in New England, labeled themselves as Federalists, no one used the term "Democrat" until the 1820s. Informed by Plato and the western tradition, wittingly or not, Americans thought the word "democrat" was synonymous with animalistic or mob passions. While democracy was a critical element of any body politic, it represented the stomach or the procreative region of the human body, devoid of reason and rationalism. Those who did not identify as Federalists prior to the 1820s almost always denoted themselves as Republicans. The problem was so many Americans called themselves Republicans—especially after the failed and seemingly treasonous Hartford Convention of 1814 that tarnished the word "Federalist"—that the term meant little.[34] Three such groups were the National Republicans, who supported government-funded public works; Old Republicans, who were more Jefferson than Jefferson and believed nothing not explicitly stated in the Constitution; and the Constitutional Republicans, who either did or did not support government-funded public works, which they believed weren't necessarily authorized by the Constitution. The tradition promoted by George Washington as well as James Monroe was strictly that a republic could not, at any level, allow for the formation of political parties. There was only the common good (res publica), and anything beyond that was corruption and decay, the beginning of the end of a republic.

According to the Schlesinger school of thought, the second party system began in 1827 with the formation of the Democratic Party and the Anti-Mason Party, which became the Whig Party in 1833. In 1854, the third party system arrived with the implosion of the Democrats and the Whigs over the issues of slavery and popular sovereignty. On this, the Schlesinger school is mostly correct, though it should have properly labeled the formation of the Democratic and Whig parties as the first "party system" rather than the second. Nothing existed in America prior to 1827 that resembled a political party in any modern or recognizable form. There is no doubt that issues—such as the Constitution, foreign relations with France and Britain, and the creation of the U.S. Bank—divided Americans. But the men of the early republic grouped together more by personalities, single issues, religious preferences, and sectional loyalties than by organized political parties. Theirs was, as legal scholar and historian Bruce Frohnen has so wisely argued, the last gasp of pre-ideological politics.

The first real political party in American history, and the one historians usually classify as Jackson's party, was the Democratic Party. It began in 1827, but it is still the same party, institutionally, that exists today. The party does not have an illustrious history, which is probably why few modern Democrats ever reference it. Under its leadership, America passed the Fugitive Slave Law in 1850, the Kansas-Nebraska Act in 1854, and the Jim Crow laws of the 1890s; re-segregated Washington, D.C., and all government offices during Woodrow Wilson's presidency; refused Jewish refugees from Europe in the 1930s; imprisoned Japanese-Americans in internment camps in World War II; and obliterated two Japanese, civilian urban centers in 1945. Not exactly a noble record of civilization, achievement, or progress. In fact, one would not be amiss in arguing that the first hundred-plus years of the Democratic Party was an era of power, rape, abuse, and murder.

It is unclear if Andrew Jackson considered the Democratic Party, or any party, a good thing for the country, despite being so intimately associated with it. During the 1828 election, some parties calling themselves "Democrats" opposed Jackson, and others that supported him went under a variety of names, such as the "People's Ticket."[35] Yet when he did speak or write on the issue of parties prior to 1830, he had nothing but contempt for them. Real republicans, he argued frequently, decided matters through principle and circumstance, not party. Jackson's closest allies felt the same. In 1830, Davy Crockett wrote, "To General Jackson I am a firm and undeviating friend. I have fought under his command—and am proud to own that he has been my commander. I have loved him, and in the sincerity of my heart I say that I still love him." However, the frontiersman and hero of the Alamo continued, "But to be compelled to love every one who, for purposes of self-aggrandizement, pretend to rally around the 'Jackson Standard,' is what I never can submit to."[36]

According to extant documents, the Democratic Party seems to have been the brainchild of three men: Martin Van Buren, John C. Calhoun, and Thomas Hart Benton.[37] Van Buren would become one of the greatest Jacksonians of his age, and Thomas Hart Benton also became a close ally of Jackson. Calhoun, however, followed his own path, using Jackson when it suited but discarding and fighting him later. The three men took advantage of the chaos created by the "corrupt bargain" to tear down the "no-party system," which began with Washington's presidency and persisted until the conclusion of Monroe's, and build the first modern party. Each contributed something unique and essential to it. Van Buren brought Machiavellian political acumen as well as money from New York bankers and financiers. Benton, less manipulative than Van Buren but possessing a frontiersman mystique combined with purpose and intelligence, brought the votes of frontier farmers, ever procreating and expanding in the West. Always brilliant but never trustworthy, Calhoun brought, at least in theory, the support of the only southerners that really mattered, the plantation owners. Together, the three believed they could use Jackson—who they were convinced was not altogether brilliant—as a symbol and rallying point for the new party. But it was not until around 1835, as Martin Van Buren prepared for the 1836 election, that something resembling the modern Democratic Party came into being, organized at every level of the republic and united by a relatively common cause.[38] Jackson avoided the term "Democrat" and referred to himself as a republican and anyone who opposed him and his allies as the "opposition."

The Old Republicans

Among Jackson's unlikely allies were the "Old Republicans," led by John Randolph of Roanoke, John Taylor of Caroline, Thomas McKean, and Nathaniel Macon. Like Jackson, they were strict constitutionalists. Unlike Jackson, they opposed the Louisiana Purchase, believing the president did not have the constitutional authority to purchase land from a foreign sovereign. Classically educated and armed with an idealized vision of the Roman Republic, they believed democracy, avarice, and power destroyed republics.

While serving in the U.S. Senate, Jackson found himself quite taken with these men and many, if not all, of their ideas. The Old Republicans liked Jackson as well. Understandably, he was not one of them, being too western, and, thus, too pro-expansion when in favor of the frontier, and not at their level of academic intelligence. But he was an ally nonetheless, a man who distrusted centralized political authority as much as they did.

Most importantly, though, the Old Republicans despised Henry Clay for his radical nationalism. Randolph even fought a duel with Clay in 1824, though neither man hurt the other, and Randolph verbally lambasted Clay whenever possible, especially over the "corrupt bargain" that had made Clay secretary of state.

By contrast, Randolph spoke of Jackson in glowing if not messianic terms. Jackson, he declared time and again on the Senate floor, was the only man who could reclaim and purify the fallen American republic. One of his speeches praising Jackson lasted close to six hours, and the official government publishers of congressional debates, allies of Clay, refused to print the speech.[39]

Even after Randolph left the Senate in 1827, he continued to support Jackson. "What I have most at heart of all attainable objects is the election of General Jackson," he wrote to the *Richmond Enquirer* in early 1828.[40] In turn, Jackson admired Randolph immensely, and, in early 1830, as president, he appointed him ambassador to Russia.

The Nashville Committee

Though Jackson had allies throughout the Union, he trusted those from Nashville, in particular, and Tennessee, in general, the most. Two of his closest allies were James K. Polk and Sam Houston, both Tennesseans. Another of his closest associates was Senator John Eaton, his chief political counselor, first biographer, and most important ally in Nashville along with Judge

John Overton, William Berkeley Lewis, and Senator Felix Grundy. These four men, known as the Nashville Committee, wealthy and dedicated, saw themselves as a republican bulwark against northeastern oppression, and they considered Andrew Jackson their national representative.

One of the first things the Nashville Committee realized was that Jackson had to present himself as an elder statesman to gain the presidency. They wanted to argue that—no longer the dueler, the militia leader, or the army major general—Jackson had grown into a republican sage, and they asked Jackson to mind his temper. Amazingly, he agreed. In 1827, Eaton warned Jackson, "be cautious—be still—be quiet; & let your friends fight the arduous battle that is before them; they will call you when wanted, & until wanted, no matter if the battle rage...lie still & sleep on, until they say to you rise up."[41] In March 1828, Eaton again warned Jackson not to let his enemies provoke him: "Leave all these matters to the judgment care and caution of your friends, and suffer nothing to [be] reached thro your writings or declarations over and about which foes may cavil, and make newspaper abuses out of, to annoy and to harass you." He continued, "This course ought to be adhered to as rigidly as tho you were the now incumbent of the office, abiding a reelection: that being the case you would maintain a rigid silence; it is no less proper as you now stand before the public to do so."[42]

On April 25, 1827, the Nashville Committee officially became the Jackson Correspondence Committee. Under the chairmanship of Judge John Overton, its "primary object the dissemination of TRUTH, and the rescue of the character of Andrew Jackson from the imputations which ignorance and political prejudice have combined to fix upon." Overton promised to answer every serious inquiry about Jackson's life and character, armed only with facts, letters of evidence, and testimonies of witnesses of the many events in the man's life. Context, he argued, mattered: whatever decisions Jackson had made as a military leader, judge, legislator, or governor had been made with the best of republican intentions.[43] In general, the Jackson Correspondence Committee served its purpose with dignity, rarely falling into mere hero worship.

Jackson's other allies, however, were not always so restrained. One group of supporters touted Andrew Jackson as "an old Tennessee farmer; the orphan child of the nation, cradled in the bosom of the Republic, reared in the camp of Mars, the soldier of the Revolution, the stern Republican, the rigid Patriot, the enlightened Statesman, the consummate General, the unprejudiced and consistent Politician, the Hero of Orleans, the veteran of two wars, the soul of his friends and the terror of his Country's enemies; possessing all the advantages of a long and active life could give to a strong and superior mind—one of us, and emphatically the People's Candidate."[44]

Jackson's Opposition

Between 1825 and 1828, Jackson's every decision, military movement, and letter became an object of close scrutiny. Certain issues, such as Jackson's treatment of deserters and his invasion of Florida, came up repeatedly during these years. Many criticisms of these issues were legitimate concerns about Jackson's character, trying to place his many violent decisions in context. His duels, of course, were common knowledge, and newspapers gleefully recounted them. Such pieces usually ended with warnings against the violence of duels, which, of course, the papers profited from retelling in gory detail. Other papers labeled Jackson a "slave trader," and several tried to claim he had been Aaron Burr's ally in committing treason against the United States.[45]

Some opposition maintained its dignity, however. The *Washington Intelligencer*, a pro-Clay and pro-Adams paper, tried to explain why Jackson's virtues might very well be his vices. "We have confined our inquiry to the public conduct of the General, and have not questioned and shall not question his motives. His violence of temper may be justly imputable to his earnest regard for right, and his hatred of wrong," the paper admitted. It continued, "the misfortune is, that, in every case of difference of opinion with every official body or person," Jackson "invariably considers himself in the right, and them, of course, in the wrong, and acts accordingly."[46] While the *Washington Intelligencer* was not entirely correct, it also was not wholly wrong. Jackson did have a tendency to see those loyal to him as absolutely right and those who disagreed with him as incorrect. As the 1828 election drew nearer, the paper continued along the same line of reasoning. No one doubted Jackson's patriotism, the paper argued, but everyone should question his lack of intelligence, insufficient for running a republic.[47]

Though rare, Jackson's opponents occasionally argued against his positions rather than his past or character. An article in the *Hagerstown Torchlight*, for example, challenged Jackson on his opposition to Clay's "American System," which funded a national system of public-works projects and supported high tariffs and banks.[48] Such rational criticism was all too scarce in the years before the 1828 election, and the same paper later wrote that Jackson could never be trusted because he was a bloodthirsty murderer, as evidenced by his duels.[49]

The strangest and most hurtful attacks Jackson endured were those against the two women he loved most. Throughout the 1820s, Rachel was accused of being a sinful woman, her character maligned after her divorce from an abusive husband. This unrelenting slur ultimately caused her heart attack in December 1828. Newspapers also launched a campaign to slander Jackson's mother. In the summer of 1828, just prior to the fall election, reports circulated that Andrew Jackson was born in 1751 or 1752, not 1765, and that his mother was a prostitute, traveling with British officers. Once they found her "used," they discarded her, and she took up with a black lover. As if to ensure no one misunderstood their point-blank insinuations, newspapers bluntly proclaimed, "JACKSON IS A MULATTO, and HIS MOTHER was a [WHORE]."[50]

It was painful for Jackson to see his pious, devout, republican, Evangelical wife denounced as reprehensible, but the vile lie that his mother, Elizabeth, was a prostitute in the service of the British devastated him. Elizabeth had lost two of her sons to the British, and she had died nursing American patriots. "My pious mother, nearly fifty years in the tomb, & who, from her cradle to her death, had not a speck upon her character," Jackson lamented in a personal letter, "held to public scorn as a prostitute." He also noted that he was at the end of his "philosophy," that is, his Stoicism was about to give way to anger and, perhaps, rage. "The day of retribution must come," he added.[51] But before his anger burst forth, tragedy struck. His beloved Rachel died four days after her heart attack.

In the face of the most vitriolic opposition campaign in American history, Andrew Jackson handily defeated John Quincy Adams in the 1828 presidential election. Jackson won fifty-six percent of the popular vote, fifteen of twenty-four states, and 178 out of 261 Electoral College votes. While Adams won all of New England, New Jersey, Delaware, and Maryland, Jackson won every western and southern state. The "Great Migration" west after the War of 1812 had radically re-oriented American politics, and Jackson, the popular embodiment of America's frontier virtues, became the first president elected by the votes of America's frontier.

Chapter Six

The World Is Governed Too Much

As a Scotch-Irish and southwestern American frontiers-man, Jackson had always held women in the highest esteem. White women, black women, Indian women—their race didn't matter to Jackson. There was something special about them, and he—an imagined and actual knight of buckskin—believed he had a duty to protect them everywhere. He had learned this from his mother, and Rachel, the abused wife of a bastard, had only strengthened his resolve on this matter. As a young man, he had invited a prostitute and her daughter to a ball. Some of Jackson's biographers have explained this as a childish prank.[1] However, given his behavior toward women of every standing throughout his life, it is far more likely that Jackson's invitation was not meant to demean but to uplift.

Jackson was beyond livid when the governor of Georgia sanctioned a massacre of Indian women and children in 1818 during the Seminole campaign of the late 1810s. "It is still more Strange that there could exist within the U. States, a cowardly monster in human Shape, that could violate the Sanctity of a flag," he wrote the governor. "Such base cowardice and murderous conduct as this transaction affords has not its paralel [sic] in history and should meet with its merited punishment."[2] For Jackson, it was one thing to meet a man, voluntarily, on the battlefield and kill him. It was quite another to attack the innocent and the defenseless.

Rachel Jackson had herself been a mortal victim of men who did not abide by Jackson's standard of chivalry. Gravely wounded by her loss, Jackson fell back on a stoic acceptance of God's will. "I bow to the decree, but feel in its afflictive power how weak are the Sentiments of Philosophy, without the aid of divine Grace," he wrote to one of Rachel's friends.[3] To William Polk, he admitted the death came as a "severe stroke" to him, but he felt assured that Rachel now resided happily in Heaven.[4] By the middle of January, Jackson was convinced that her death only strengthened his own faith to live according to "her virtues, her piety, & Christianity,"[5] and it is true that his Presbyterian faith grew far more pronounced after Rachel's death.

The *Nashville Republican* editorialized, "In the character of this excellent and lamented lady," Rachel Jackson, "feminine

charms, domestic virtues, and Christian perfections were united."
Yet, the paper chided, Andrew Jackson's enemies were responsible
for her premature death. "In order to obstruct his just popularity,
and rightful power, she was made the object of injuries more
barbarous than murderous savages could inflict," the paper continued. "And Providence after permitting her to witness the downfall and confusion of those he patronized and those who
committed these atrocities, gently withdrew her wounded spirit
to the mansions of eternal bliss."[6]

Arriving in Washington in January, hoping to meet with the
president-elect, newspaper owner Amos Kendall wrote to his
wife, "Since the news of Mrs. Jackson's death, I have less incli-
nation" to wait for his arrival. "That melancholy event will cast
a gloom over everything."[7] The *Adams Sentinel* also wondered
what all of this might mean. "At the moment of his high eleva-
tion, he is suddenly depressed and cast down. His hopes are
disappointed, his plans deranged. Just as he is about to feel the
weight of new cares, responsibilities and duties, he is deprived
of domestic solace."[8] But Jackson's sense of duty remained
strong. He arrived with his Tennessee entourage in Hagerstown,
Maryland, on February 8, and his admirers rushed "forward to
greet him, not as a conquering hero, but as a plain republican
citizen." One paper noted, "The frosts and cares of sixty win-
ters" and the recent death of his wife "have silvered his locks,
but his step is still that of a weather beaten soldier, firm and
elastic."[9]

The Cabinet and the Petticoats

After becoming a newly elected president, Jackson's most difficult initial challenge was to form a cabinet and staff his government. As someone who believed that Washington, D.C., was a modern Sodom, full of corruption, laziness, and manipulative bureaucrats, he had a major chore ahead of him.[10] Jackson was exceedingly scrupulous in his desire to stamp out government malfeasance. "Corruption in some and in others [is] a perversion of correct feelings and principles," Jackson explained, "divert government from its legitimate ends and make it an engine for the support of the few at the expense of the many."[11] Jackson believed that limited government, especially at the federal level, was a good not only in itself, respectful of the Constitution and free men, but also necessary to prevent bureaucratic venality. He disliked taxes, debt, tariffs, and a standing army, and he wanted a cabinet that reflected these views—men dedicated to rooting out corruption, reducing expenditures, and being worthy of his and the public's trust.

Consequently, Jackson's cabinet reflected his friendships more than anything else. Previous cabinets had reflected sectional differences in the country, an attempt by the previous six presidents to foster national harmony and unity. Cabinet members were often well-known political figures. But Jackson was an outsider, distrusted by many in Washington, and his opponents were vitriolic against him. "If any other President had committed half the outrages on the Constitution, and on the liberties and feelings of his countrymen, that Gen. Jackson has, that president would, ere this, have been numbered, by impartial history, with the tyrants by whom mankind have been oppressed," railed the *Hagerstown Torchlight*, which accused him of promoting "his most obnoxious minions"[12] to government office.

Jackson's first cabinet consisted, naturally, of some of his closest allies. He named New York's Martin Van Buren as secretary of state, John Henry Eaton as secretary of war, Senator John Branch of North Carolina as secretary of the navy, Senator John M. Berrien of Georgia as attorney general, and Congressman Samuel D. Ingham of Pennsylvania as secretary of the Treasury. Perhaps most interesting, he nominated Adams's Postmaster General John McLean, an opponent of slavery, to the Supreme Court and appointed William T. Barry, former secretary of state of Kentucky, as the new postmaster general.[13]

Even Van Buren found this cabinet bizarre. "There was probably not one of these malcontents [Jackson's opponents] more disappointed than myself by the composition of the administration,"[14] Van Buren admitted in his autobiography. While each of these men was loyal to Jackson, they offered him nothing in terms of political gain, and, in fact, a cabinet member soon plunged him into controversy.

John Eaton, soon to be appointed secretary of war, had recently married Peggy O'Neale, a widowed pub and hotel owner. She was extremely charismatic and intelligent but also idiosyncratic and regarded as somewhat trashy by Washington society, and she was a Roman Catholic. Her first husband, John

B. Timberlake, had died while on naval service in the Mediterranean—a post acquired for him by Eaton, who had also retired Timberlake's substantial debts as a favor to the couple, with whom he was friendly.

Though medical examiners concluded that Timberlake died of pneumonia, Washington gossips spread the rumor that he had committed suicide because Eaton was having an affair with his wife. The rumor gained greater currency after Eaton and Peggy O'Neale married less than a year later.

President Jackson liked the young couple, but Vice President John C. Calhoun's wife, Floride, the wives of the other cabinet secretaries, and other Washington society ladies ("the petticoats") refused to associate with her. The naturally chivalrous Jackson sympathized with the Eatons, especially given his own experience with malicious gossips, but without Rachel's guidance he was at a loss about how to reconcile the members of his cabinet. "You will receive that heartfelt welcome that you were ever wont to do, when my D[ea]r departed wife was living—her absence makes every thing here wear to me a gloomy & melancholy aspect," he admitted to Eaton in the midst of the scandal.[15]

"I believe no lady has been more basely slandered, or cruelly persecuted than Mrs. Eaton," Jackson told Stephen Decatur's wife. "I have heard much said to her prejudice, but no one has even yet had the hardihood to say to me that he or she, of their own knowledge, knew any thing against her, as a moral virtuous and correct woman."[16]

In the course of the Eaton scandal, Jackson's closest friends and allies turned against each other—the secretary of war even challenged the secretary of the Treasury to a duel on the streets of Washington, D.C. Jackson found the whole episode deeply depressing and restructured his cabinet in 1831. Postmaster General William T. Barry, who sided with Jackson and the Eatons, was the only holdover.[17] Jackson made a recess appointment of Martin Van Buren—who stayed loyal to Jackson and the Eatons and was himself a widower—as America's ambassador (or minister) to the Court of St. James's in Britain, and he made John Eaton the governor of Florida and then the ambassador to Spain.[18] Vice President John C. Calhoun used his influence in the Senate to reject Van Buren's appointment, but Van Buren got the last laugh by eventually becoming Jackson's vice president and successor.

For his second cabinet, Jackson chose Maryland's Roger B. Taney to serve briefly as his secretary of war (Taney thus became the first Catholic appointed to a federal cabinet position) before nominating him as the eleventh attorney general of the United States. Governor Lewis Cass of Michigan became the next secretary of war, replacing Taney, and Louis McLane, a former U.S. senator from Delaware and ambassador to Britain, was appointed secretary of the Treasury. Levi Woodbury, a former governor of New Hampshire, was installed as secretary of the Navy, and U.S. Senator Edward Livingston of Louisiana was made secretary of state.

The Ultimate Jacksonian Man: Amos Kendall

Almost as important as his official cabinet was Jackson's unofficial "kitchen cabinet" led by Amos Kendall, a steadfast Jackson friend and ally from 1829. Kendall had graduated first in his class from Dartmouth College in 1811 then moved to Kentucky where he became a lawyer, writer, publisher, and proponent of Jacksonian republicanism. When Kendall first arrived in Washington in January 1829, he, like Jackson, viewed the city as a cesspool of corruption:

> On the whole, if there is more extravagance, folly, and corruption anywhere in the world than in this city, I do not wish to see that place. People of moderate income attempt to imitate foreign ministers, the President, and secretaries, and thus keep themselves poor, when by prudence and economy they might make ample provision for their families. There is great room for reform here in almost every respect, and I hope Jackson and his friends will introduce it.[19]

When he and Jackson met, they liked one another immediately. Jackson offered him a position at the Department of the Treasury, directing him to ferret out corruption, and Kendall threw himself into the work of reform:[20]

> God knows when I shall get away from here. These investigations into the conduct of the men lately in

office are so important that they must be made completed as soon as possible, that the government may
recover the money out of which it has been cheated. I
have discovered frauds in Dr. Watkins, who went
before me in this office, to the amount of more than
$7,000, and how much more will come to light I know
not.[21]

Kendall spent as much time firing bureaucrats as he did inves-
tigating fraud and gaining repayment to the Treasury.[22] Overall,
Kendall estimated, Jackson and his officers removed roughly one
out of every seven government bureaucrats between 1829 and
1832, "most of them for bad conduct and character."[23] The Jacksonians referred to this as "rotation" while the enemies of Jackson
called it "spoils."[24] Kendall estimated that the customs houses were
responsible for the greatest fraud, at roughly $280,000, with fish-
ing bounties amounting to more than $51,000.[25] He also identified
additional fraud in the navy. Though a friendly and congenial man,
Kendall knew that his reforms led to few friendships:

Sometimes my associates in the government would
allude with a sort of sarcastic pleasantry to my scrupu-
lousness on that subject, and my uniform reply was in
substance that I did not set myself up as a censor or
judge of other men's conduct or consciences in the exercise of their special privileges; but for myself I deemed
it the safest rule to keep within the limits of the law.[26]

For those serving directly under him, Kendall established eight rules of conduct. First, every government officer must begin work by 9:00 a.m. and not end until 3:00 p.m. Second, should society need an officer to work past 3:00 p.m., he must. Third, no officer could read a book or newspaper during working hours unless absolutely necessary for the job at hand. Fourth, any gambling or drunkenness during or out of office hours would result in immediate dismissal. Fifth, the acceptance of any gratuity would also result in immediate dismissal. Sixth, no details about any investigation could ever be made public. Seven, no officer could accept a second job. And, finally, no officer could use any office supplies for anything other than government business.[27]

Kendall represented the spirit of Jacksonian reform. He later served in the Van Buren administration as postmaster general, helped build Baptist churches, and co-founded the national university for the deaf, Gallaudet University.

Indian Removal

In 1969, when the New Left attacked Jackson, Dr. Francis Paul Prucha, a professor of American history—and a Jesuit priest who would be nominated for a Pulitzer Prize in 1985 for his book *The Great Father: The United States Government and the American Indians*—dismissed the New Left's "devil theory" of history, which substituted people like Jackson for Satan. "Although his years in the West had brought him into frequent contact with the

Indians, he by no means developed a doctrinaire anti-Indian attitude," Prucha wrote in response to New Left attacks on Jackson. "Rather, as a military man, his dominant goal was to preserve the security and well-being of the United States and its Indian and white inhabitants."[28]

Whatever the controversies, two things can be definitively stated about Jackson and Indian removal. First, Jackson was in no way a racist. He believed Indians were people created by God and inherently equal to whites, even if he also believed that Indian civilization lagged behind.[29] Second, he firmly believed that Indian removal served the interests of both the Indians and the white settlers who would otherwise come into conflict—one that the Indians would surely lose—with each other. Jackson knew that whites all too frequently mistreated the Indians.

> It has long been the policy of government to introduce among them [the Indians] the arts of civilization, in the hope of gradually reclaiming them from a wandering life. This policy has, however, been coupled with another wholly incompatible with its success. Professing a desire to civilize and settle them, we have at the same time lost no opportunity to purchase their lands and thrust them farther into the wilderness. By this means they have not only been kept in a wandering state, but been led to look upon us as unjust and indifferent to their fate.[30]

For Jackson, there also was a constitutional issue. He did not believe that the Indian tribes could exist as sovereign nations within the several sovereign states of the Union. There could not be separate laws for the people of Georgia, for instance, and for tribes living within Georgia's boundaries. If the tribes were to remain sovereign, if they were to govern themselves according to their own tribal rules and customs and laws, they had to be re-established in lands set aside for them and not within the confines of an existing state of the United States. Removing the American Indians to a "Permanent Indian Frontier" (the ninety-fifth meridian, roughly where Kansas City is) would, Jackson hoped, take Indians out of the path of frontier settlement and allow them to go their own way.[31]

> As a means of effecting this end I suggest for your con-
> sideration the propriety of setting apart an ample dis-
> trict west of the Mississippi, and without the limits of
> any state or territory now formed, to be guaranteed to
> the Indian tribes as long as they shall occupy it, each
> tribe having a distinct control over the portion desig-
> nated for its use. There they may be secured in the
> enjoyment of governments of their own choice, subject
> to no other control from the United States than such as
> may be necessary to preserve peace on the frontier and
> between the several tribes. There the benevolent may
> endeavor to teach them the arts of civilization, and, by

promoting union and harmony among them, to raise
up an interesting commonwealth, destined to perpetuate the race and to attest the humanity and justice of
this government.[32]

Jackson's policy was controversial in his own time, but he was
able to get the Indian Removal Act passed in the House by 101
votes to 97 and in the Senate by 28 votes to 19 and signed into
law in late May 1830.[33] Jackson considered it a hallmark piece of
legislation and a seminal part of his presidency.

Jackson's Indian removal policy as implemented, however,
was a humanitarian disaster, as the visiting Alexis de Tocqueville
noted:

At the end of the year 1831, I found myself on the left
bank of the Mississippi, at a place named Memphis by
the Europeans. While I was in this place, a numerous
troop of Choctaws (the French of Louisiana call
them *Chactas*) came; these savages left their country
and tried to pass to the right bank of the Mississippi
where they flattered themselves about finding a refuge
that the American government had promised them. It
was then the heart of winter, and the cold gripped that
year with unaccustomed intensity; snow had hardened
on the ground, and the river swept along enormous
chunks of ice. The Indians led their families with them;

they dragged along behind them the wounded, the sick, the newborn children, the elderly about to die. They had neither tents nor wagons, but only a few provisions and weapons. I saw them embark to cross the great river, and this solemn spectacle will never leave my memory. You heard among this assembled crowd neither sobs nor complaints; they kept quiet. Their misfortunes were old and seemed to them without remedy. All the Indians had already entered the vessel that was to carry them; their dogs still remained on the bank; when these animals saw finally that their masters were going away forever, they let out dreadful howls, and throwing themselves at the same time into the icy waters of the Mississippi, they swam after their masters.[34]

For good reason, Tocqueville looked upon the scene with disgust and pity. Though he had come to America ostensibly to study its prison system, he instead spent most of his time studying the first modern republic, which he hoped would be humanity's future. But this, the coerced removal of entire peoples, represented the worst of American democracy. Thousands of Indians—Cherokees, Chickasaw, Creeks, Seminoles, and Choctaws—died on the "Trail of Tears." More died from disease—cholera, malaria, small pox, and influenza—once they reached what is now Oklahoma.

"We did not visit a house, wigwam, or camp," wrote a distressed missionary to the Choctaws, "where we did not find more or less sickness, and in most instances the whole family were prostrated by disease. Great numbers of them have died." The sickness hit the children hardest, and child mortality rates soared. The missionaries were unable to report that "births decidedly outnumber the deaths" until 1855. By 1860, the Choctaw population stood at 13,666, a 27 percent decline from 1831.[35] Tocqueville thought that there was no greater example of American hypocrisy than the way democratic Americans condemned autocratic Spain for its mistreatment of the Indians while simultaneously taking pride in America's policy of "calmly, legally, philanthropically" destroying "men while [allegedly] better respecting the laws of humanity...."[36] Jackson was a hypocrite in very little. And if this was hypocrisy, it was a hypocrisy he shared with his fellow frontiersmen.

Robert V. Remini, however, denies that Jackson was a hypocrite—arguing instead that he was a realist. Remini writes that "many of the qualities that made" Jackson "a great general also aided him in becoming a great President. For decades his predecessors faced the problem of dealing with unrelenting clashes between whites and Native Americans. The first thing Jackson as President accomplished was passage of the Indian Removal Act over stiff congressional opposition. The Trail of Tears was a terrible price to pay for this legislation, but, as Jackson predicted, the Cherokee, Chickasaw, Creek, Choctaws, and Seminole tribes are alive today. They were not annihilated like the Yamasee, Mohawks and Pequots, and other eastern tribes."[37]

Political Economy

If his policy of Indian removal was heavy-handed or brutal, Jackson's economic policies were what we might call "libertarian." He disapproved of federal intervention in the economy, thinking that if any intervention should be done, it should be done in a limited way by the states. Jackson opposed, for the most part, tariffs, taxes, and federal spending on "internal improvements." He supported small government, balanced budgets, and abolishing the federal debt—a feat he achieved, and one that no other president has accomplished.

Francis Blair, founding editor of *The Globe* and a member of Jackson's kitchen cabinet, summarized Jacksonian economic theory in the newspaper's masthead with the following motto: "The world is governed too much."[38] In Jacksonian economic theory, workers and manufacturers were "producers," bureaucrats and bankers were "parasites," and a republican people should be left to look after itself with voluntary associations of the sort that Alexis de Tocqueville thought were part of the unique and powerful character of America. As Tocqueville wrote in a famous passage,

> Americans of all ages, all stations in life, and all types
> of disposition are forever forming associations. There

are not only commercial and industrial associations in which all take part, but others of a thousand different types—religious, moral, serious, futile, very general and very limited, immensely large and very minute. Americans combine to give fêtes, found seminaries, build churches, distribute books, and send missionaries to the antipodes. Hospitals, prisons, and schools take shape in that way. Finally, if they want to proclaim a truth or propagate some feeling by the encouragement of a great example, they form an association. In every case, as the head of any new undertaking, where in France you would find the government or in England some territorial magnate, in the United States you are sure to find an association.[39]

Two battles—each waged and won—reveal much about Jackson's understanding of the federal government's role in the economy. In 1830, Jackson vetoed the Maysville Road Bill, which appropriated federal monies to Maryland for internal improvements. In his veto message, Jackson stressed that while the Constitution did not expressly forbid the use of federal monies for local purposes, it seemed clear that the founders did not intend for such funds to be appropriated to the states in that way. In a private letter to John Overton, Jackson complained that

"[Henry] Clay, in his American System, lays it down, that congress has the constitutional power to make roads and canals, without limitation.... The internal improvement mania pervades congress, the log rolling principles has fully displayed itself."[40] The idea that the federal government might use the public Treasury to fund or purchase stock options seemed especially abhorrent to Jackson. If the federal government ever assumed such powers, "Where would you stop," the president asked, "would the people suffer themselves to be taxed for such purposes—would not such a power be too dangerous to your liberties." Federal monies, Jackson argued, could be justly appropriated only for undertakings that benefitted the entire nation.[41] Jackson's veto shocked many. The *Hagerstown Torchlight* complained that Jackson cared more about the American Indians—for whom he had just allocated millions of dollars in the Indian Removal Act—than he did about Maryland's citizens. "The United States' Treasury cannot spare $90,000 for the Rockville Road," the paper argued, "but the people of Maryland must spare six hundred and fifty-two thousand dollars for the removal of the Indians."[42]

The second great battle Jackson and the Jacksonians waged was against the Second Bank of the United States. The bank had been chartered in 1816 at a value of $35 million as a public-private corporation—an alliance that seemed unholy to Jackson and his followers. "Were all the worshippers of the gold Calf to memorialize me and request a restoration of the Deposits," he reportedly said to Martin Van Buren, "I would cut off my right hand from my body before I would do such an act. The golden calf may be worshipped by others but as for myself I serve the Lord."⁴³ For Jackson, economics was as much about morality as it was about efficiency and progress. So, by that measure, by what constitutional power did the bank even exist? If it was public, keep it public for the benefit of all. If private, let it remain private. As Jackson viewed it, the bank was nothing less than a conspiracy to arm and empower an American economic aristocracy, concentrating power in the Northeast against the interests of the West and the South. Behind all of Jackson's arguments, though, lurked the traditional agrarian view that bankers produced nothing of value. The entire banking system, especially if not backed by gold or silver, was a con game that took money from hard-working producers and gave it to men who did nothing but push paper. Jackson's veto message bled anger:

> It is to be regretted that the rich and powerful too often bend the acts of government to their selfish purposes. Distinctions in society will always exist under every just government. Equality of talents, of education, or of wealth can not be produced by human institutions. In the full enjoyment of the gifts of Heaven and the fruits of superior industry, economy, and virtue, every man is equally entitled to protection by law; but when the laws undertake to add to these natural and just advantages artificial distinctions, to grant titles, gratuities, and exclusive privileges, to make the

rich richer and the potent more powerful, the humble members of society-the farmers, mechanics, and laborers-who have neither the time nor the means of securing like favors to themselves, have a right to complain of the injustice of their Government. There are no necessary evils in government. Its evils exist only in its abuses. If it would confine itself to equal protection, and, as Heaven does its rains, shower its favors alike on the high and the low, the rich and the poor, it would be an unqualified blessing. In the act before me there seems to be a wide and unnecessary departure from these just principles.[44]

When private interests use public monies, they do so for their own self-aggrandizement, Jackson argued, and the bank wielded unjust power over every American forced to pay for it.

Is there no danger to our liberty and independence in a bank that in its nature has so little to bind it to our country? The president of the bank has told us that most of the State banks exist by its forbearance. Should its influence become concentered, as it may under the operation of such an act as this, in the hands of a self-elected directory whose interests are identified with those of the foreign stockholders, will there not be cause to tremble for the purity of our elections in peace and for the independence of our country in war? Their power would be great whenever they might choose to exert it; but if this monopoly were regularly renewed every fifteen or twenty years on terms proposed by themselves, they might seldom in peace put forth their strength to influence elections or control the affairs of the nation. But if any private citizen or public functionary should interpose to curtail its powers or prevent a renewal of its privileges, it can not be doubted that he would be made to feel its influence.[45]

Moreover, the bank had failed at its presumed purpose of making the economy more efficient. Jackson believed it was responsible for the Panic of 1819, during which recalled loans led to bank failures, bankruptcies, and what would later be called inflation. Many investors in the bank were British, which also did not endear the bank to the president. "My dear Sir cut the Lilliputian ties that entangle you. Refuse any bank Bill that does not open the stock to all of us," John Randolph advised. "Shall we be tributary to English stockholders...."[46]

Jackson vetoed the rechartering of the bank (which was due to expire in 1836), and he resolved to abolish it completely before the end of his second term as president. He largely succeeded, removing federal deposits and shearing the bank of its regulatory power so that it was privatized in 1836, near the end of Jackson's second term, and dissolved completely in 1841.

The combination of Jacksonian economic policies helped create an economy that boomed for almost two decades prior to the American Civil War.[47] Still, the battles Jackson and his supporters waged against the U.S. Bank, taxes, and corruption were minor compared to the war he would wage against the Nullifiers, who said that states could nullify federal laws. Jackson supported states' rights, but he saw in the doctrine of nullification a mortal threat to the American Republic.

Chapter Seven

Nullifying the Nullifiers

A s far back as records indicate, Andrew Jackson supported the Union but never nationalism. He believed in the Union's inviolability, but he accepted that within it a significant decentralization, disunity, and competition must and should exist. Jackson also believed in what a modern Catholic would call a principle of "subsidiarity," which claims that the power responsible for ameliorating a problem in society is whichever authority is closest to the issue, allowing for proper order. A true republican, Jackson maintained that the division of powers happened not just vertically among the three branches of the federal government, but also vertically and horizontally among all the nation's associations and branches. And the Union's primary purpose was to protect these millions of associations—families, schools, businesses, clubs, churches, or states—that existed in a polycentric fashion within the republic. Jackson's preference for militias over a standing army beautifully illustrates his approach to this flowchart of responsibilities. He wanted to keep authority and its exercise at the most immediate and local level, trusting that free men would sacrifice themselves for the greatest duties of hearth and home when called upon.

Not everyone agreed with Jackson's idealistic views about the proper division of power and the Union's chief objective. In 1830, in one of his most famous speeches, Senator Daniel Webster of Massachusetts declared,

> While the Union lasts, we have high, exciting, gratifying prospects spread out before us, for us and our children. Beyond that I seek not to penetrate the veil. God grant that, in my day, at least, that curtain may not rise. God grant that on my vision never may be opened what lies behind. When my eyes shall be turned to behold, for the last time, the sun in Heaven, may I not see him shining on the broken and dishonored fragments of a once glorious Union; on States dissevered, discordant, belligerent; on a land rent with civil feuds, or drenched, it may be, in fraternal blood! Let their last feeble and lingering glance, rather behold the gorgeous Ensign of

the Republic, now known and honored throughout the earth, still full high advanced, its arms and trophies streaming in their original lustre, not a stripe erased or polluted, nor a single star obscured—bearing for its motto, no such miserable interrogatory as, *What is all this worth?* Nor those other words of delusion and folly, *Liberty first, and Union afterward*—but every where, spread all over in characters of living light, blazing on all its ample folds, as they float over the sea and over the land, and in every wind under the whole Heavens, that other sentiment, dear to every true American heart—Liberty *and* Union, now and forever, one and inseparable![1]

Though Andrew Jackson thought little of Daniel Webster, he approved of this sentiment. That same year, at the Jefferson Day Dinner on April 13, Jackson offered the toast, "Our Federal Union—it must be preserved."[2] This was no pro forma declaration. South Carolina had threatened to nullify (or not enforce) the federal tariff passed by Congress in 1828, and southern statesmen, led by John C. Calhoun, were propounding a theory of state "nullification" of federal law as a necessary check on federal power. Many saw in this the unraveling of the Union.

"Of your re-election there can be no doubt," John Randolph of Roanoke assured President Jackson in 1832, "but it will be to rule over a dismembered Empire."[3] Randolph, though a friend of

Jackson and an enemy of Calhoun, believed fundamentally in the right of a state to resist federal encroachment, and he told Jackson, "I am resolute not to assist in the subjugation of South Carolina, but if she does move (as I fear she will)." He insisted he would join in "common cause with [South Carolina] against the usurpations of the Federal Govt. & of the Supreme Court especially."[4]

A Union Man

Though he believed in states' rights nearly as much as Randolph, Andrew Jackson was a steadfast "union man." To understand the nullification debate he faced, one needs to remember that, prior to the American Civil War, debating the meaning of "the Union," nationhood, state sovereignty, *imperium in imperio* (sovereignty within sovereignty), and the role of checks and balances (not only within the federal government but also between the federal government and the states) was as American as apple pie.

At least from the time of the Declaration of Independence—which declared "That these United Colonies are, and of Right ought to be Free and Independent States"—Americans, while recognizing that they had inherited the rights of Englishmen as a birth right, saw their real sovereignty as residing within their individual states (or colonial assemblies) rather than with Parliament in England. Article II of the Articles of Confederation, the first governing charter of the new American union, promised that "each state retains its sovereignty, freedom and independence, and every Power, Jurisdiction and right, which is not by this confederation expressly delegated to the United States, in Congress assembled."[5] As the great historian Forrest McDonald wrote, "Patriots of all stripes accepted the primacy of the states as a fact of political life, but they were far from unanimously happy about it."[6]

It was this unhappiness that led, in 1787, to a constitutional convention to revise the Articles of Confederation. Decisions at the convention were made on the basis of each state having one vote.[7] The resulting Constitution then had to be approved by each state in its own constitutional convention.[8] The United States were referred to, at this time, in the plural, not the singular.[9]

One of the chief points of contention in the ratification debates was whether it was necessary to create a stronger federal government to pursue the primary purpose of government—justice—or whether a stronger federal government would create a centralized state that benefited only the well-connected and their cronies. It is clear that Jackson, like many of his contemporaries, partook of both these views. He believed in the strong use of his executive power as president to pursue justice under the Constitution, and he had simultaneously always been, and remained, a proponent of limited federal power.

Pro-nationalist feeling ran high after the War of 1812. It was then that President James Madison promoted the creation of a Second Bank of the United States, claiming it to be "the general will of the people."[10] Henry Clay promoted the "American System" to bolster tariffs and fund massive internal improvements, and, ironically, South Carolinian statesman John C. Calhoun backed him up.

> Let it not be forgotten, let it be forever kept in mind, that the extent of the republic exposes us to the greatest of calamities–disunion. We are great, and rapidly–I was about to say fearfully–growing. This is our pride and danger, our weakness and our strength.... We are under the most imperious obligations to counteract every tendency to disunion.... Whatever impedes the intercourse of the extremes with this, the centre of the republic, weakens the union.... Let us, then, bind the republic together with a perfect system of roads and canals. Let us conquer space. [11]

In the course of events, Jackson's enemy, Congressman Henry Clay, would become his partial ally, and John C. Calhoun, Jackson's vice president, would become his main enemy. Indeed, the South Carolinian fomented the very disunion he earlier claimed to fear.

The Enemy Within

Calhoun was duplicitous, and Jackson, who was not, had a hard time understanding this fact. It was not until May 1830—when Jackson came across evidence that Calhoun had wanted him arrested on charges of treason during the 1818 Seminole campaign—that President Jackson realized his vice president, who pretended to be his ally, was actually a long-standing, behind-the-scenes enemy. When he learned that Calhoun had been deceiving him for more than a decade, he was, understandably, depressed and furious. He wrote Calhoun seeking an explanation. "That frankness which I trust has always characterized me thro' life, toward those with whom I have been in habits of friendship induces me to lay before you the enclosed copy" of the evidence that, despite Calhoun's professions of support, Calhoun had used to undermine Jackson in the Seminole campaign. "My object in making this communication is to announce to you the great surprise which is felt, and to learn of you whether it be possible that the information given is correct."[12] In his response on May 29, 1830, Calhoun made no apologies but rather expressed contempt that Jackson had only now realized Calhoun's views from 1818. Then, in typical Calhoun fashion, he attempted to justify his actions at great length.[13] Jackson responded with a swift cut. Calhoun clearly misunderstood the purpose of Jackson's letter. It was merely to state, "et tu Brute."[14]

Calhoun's Theory

Calhoun's animosity toward Jackson had, if anything, only grown worse. He had regarded Jackson as an ignorant tool to be used by a clever man like himself. But now Jackson and Calhoun were open political opponents in a fundamental, constitutional battle. In fact, in the first half of the nineteenth century, the two most important political figures—touchstones, really—were Andrew Jackson and John C. Calhoun.

In South Carolina, Calhoun's prestige was second only to George Washington, and Calhoun, to be sure, was a fascinating, complex figure and a first-rate American thinker. During his impressive career, he had served as secretary of war, vice president, and U.S. senator. His thought, though, evolved considerably over his adult career. Prior to the Missouri Compromise of 1820, Calhoun had been a war hawk and a nationalist. But the debates surrounding the admission of Missouri as a slave state or a free state shocked Calhoun, as they shocked many Americans, who suddenly realized how divided the country had become over the issue of slavery. For Calhoun, the issue suddenly became not national unity, but protecting the South from a stridently abolitionist North.

Calhoun's classic political statement is his essay "A Disquisition on Government" (1851). He begins by denying that man ever lived in a state of nature:

> It never did, nor can exist; as it is inconsistent with the preservation and perpetuation of the race. It is, therefore, a great misnomer to call it *the state of nature.* Instead of being the natural state of man, it is, of all conceivable states, the most opposed to his nature— most repugnant to his feelings, and most incompatible with his wants.[15]

Our political life instead comes from the Garden of Eden and the idea of just authority. Men are not born into a state of nature; they are born into a family, a community, a society, a culture, and a nation. Because of the Fall, men tend toward "a universal state of conflict, between individual and individual; accompanied by the connected passions of suspicion, jealousy, anger, and revenge— followed by insolence, fraud and cruelty—and, if not prevented by some controlling power, ending in a state of universal discord and confusion, destructive of the social state and the ends for which it is ordained," Calhoun wrote. Something, then, must have a final authority over fallen man. Community, by its very nature, can attenuate the brutal and passionate side of man, but only to a certain degree. He must be controlled. "This controlling power," Calhoun argued, "wherever vested, or by whomsoever exercised, is GOVERNMENT."[16] While liberty is a powerful good, Calhoun believed, protection and perpetuation of the community are higher goods. Government, then, must first protect life and establish a strong order. Only later should government protect liberty. "Liberty must, and ever ought, to yield to protection; as the existence of the race is of greater moment than its improvement," Calhoun wrote.[17] Further, governments have no right to grant liberty, as liberty "is a reward to be earned, not a blessing to be gratuitously lavished on all alike." It is "a reward reserved for the intelligent, the patriotic, the virtuous and deserving."[18]

Because men behave poorly and because power almost always corrupts the human soul, checks must be placed on those running the government. Such checks on power, Calhoun contended, are called "constitutional." "Having its origin in the same principle of our nature, *constitution* stands to *government*, as *government* stands to *society*," Calhoun explained.[19] Constitution means body, and it is, therefore, organic and reflective of nature. It is not simply a product of the mind of man, but it is man's job to perfect it to the best of his abilities. "Constitution is the contrivance of man," Calhoun wrote, "while government is of Divine ordination. Man is left to perfect what the wisdom of the Infinite ordained, as necessary to preserve the race."[20] No real harmony or progress can exist without an effective constitution, for government without checks easily becomes disordered and despotic. A constitution, or "organism," as Calhoun sometimes called it, can only be effective if power opposes power and tendency opposes tendency.

For a constitution to work properly, therefore, it must take into account not only the strengths and follies of individuals but also the varying interests of communities. It follows then that a constitution cannot treat all individuals or communities equally, for individuals and communities, by their respective natures, are unique and particular. A constitution must also prevent one community or collection of communities from gaining the levers of power and oppressing the others. Suffrage alone will not protect the minority from the majority. "This radical error," as Calhoun labeled it, has been the real downfall of popular government throughout the history of western civilization. Instead, a proper constitution must combine suffrage with the "sense of each interest." This, in effect, would be a constitution working properly against a government. The sense of each interest "is neither to supersede nor diminish the importance of the right of suffrage; but to aid and perfect it."[21] Calhoun wrote,

It is manifest, that this provision must be of a character calculated to prevent any one interest, or combination of interests, from using the powers of government to aggrandize itself at the expense of the others. Here lies the evil: and just in proportion as it shall prevent, or fail to prevent it, in the same degree it will effect, or fail to effect the end intended to be accomplished. There is but one certain mode in which this result can be secured; and that is, by the adoption of some restriction or limitation, which shall so effectually prevent any one interest, or combination of interests, from obtaining the exclusive control of the government, as to render hopeless all attempts directed to that end. There is, again, but one mode in which this can be effected; and this is, by taking the sense of each interest or portion of the community, which may be unequally and injuriously affected by the action of the government, separately, through its own majority, or in some way by which its voice may be fairly expressed; and to require the consent of each interest, either to put or to keep the government in action.[22]

By community, Calhoun here means state. Each state, through its conventions, ratified the U.S. Constitution. Should it so choose, a state, according to Calhoun, has the right to exit the United States if it believes its interests are oppressed or even threatened to be oppressed.

Because the numerical majority will do almost anything—sometimes out of habit, sometimes out of ignorance, and sometimes maliciously—to protect itself and avoid restriction, the minority community or communities must have power to oppose the majority power. A proper constitution must "give to each interest or portion of the community a negative on the others," Calhoun argued. "It is this mutual negative among its various conflicting interests, which invests each with the power of protecting itself—and places the rights and safety of each where only they can be securely placed, under its own guardianship." Such a negative would be a "veto, interposition, nullification, check, or balance of power." Without such a negative power to work against it, a government will replace a constitution, resulting in an unnatural and improper consolidation of society. And, with the consolidation of the unchecked government, the only form of resistance left to any opposition will be violence. Most possibly, Calhoun feared, violence could lead to "anarchy, the greatest of all evils."[23] The ultimate result of rule by suffrage alone, Calhoun concluded, is chaos and division. A constitution that embraces the numerical majority and the rights of communities—what Calhoun labeled the "concurrent majority"—leads to compromise, harmony, and social stability. "The concurrent majority, on the other hand, tends to unite the most opposite and conflicting interests, and to blend the whole in one common attachment to the country," he concluded. "By giving to each interest, or portion, the power of self-protection, all strife and struggle between them for ascendancy, is prevented," and the society as a whole works for "patriotism, nationality, harmony, and a struggle only for supremacy in promoting the common good of the whole."[24]

Such was the distillation of Calhoun's political thought, which was well developed by the time of the nullification crisis—hugely influential in his native state and shaped by the profound divisions already present in the Union.

The Crisis

South Carolina had been livid since the 1828 "Tariff of Abominations," which it felt was grossly unfair to southern states that exported cotton and other agricultural goods in exchange for European imports. For the next four years, Calhoun and his state's politicians said that if the federal government did not repeal the tariff, South Carolina would nullify it. In 1832, Jackson signed a compromise tariff bill. But it was not enough to placate Calhoun, who had resigned as vice president to fight for his state and his fellow South Carolinians as a U.S. senator. On November 24, 1832, a South Carolina convention nullified the federal tariff. Its statement was simple and direct.

We, therefore, the people of the State of South Carolina, in convention assembled, do declare and ordain
and it is hereby declared and ordained, that the several
acts and parts of acts of the Congress of the United
States, purporting to be laws for the imposing of duties
and imposts on the importation of foreign commodi-
ties, and now having actual operation and effect within
the United States, and, more especially, an act entitled
"An act in alteration of the several acts imposing duties
on imports," approved on the nineteenth day of May,
one thousand eight hundred and twenty-eight, and also
an act entitled "An act to alter and amend the several
acts imposing duties on imports," approved on the
fourteenth day of July, one thousand eight hundred and
thirty-two, are unauthorized by the constitution of the
United States, and violate the true meaning and intent
thereof and are null, void, and no law, nor binding
upon this State, its officers or citizens; and all promises,
contracts, and obligations, made or entered into, or to
be made or entered into, with purpose to secure the
duties imposed by said acts, and all judicial proceedings
which shall be hereafter had in affirmance thereof, are
and shall be held utterly null and void.

Jackson, having arranged a compromise on the tariff, was
convinced that this was not the real issue for the nullifiers.[25] He

thought their real goal was the dissolution of the Union,[26] and he believed a strong response necessary.[27] On December 10, 1832, he issued his "Nullification Proclamation." "I consider, then, the power to annul a law of the United States, assumed by one State, *incompatible with the existence of the Union, contradicted expressly by the letter of the Constitution, unauthorized by its spirit, inconsistent with every principle on which it was founded, and destructive of the great object for which it was formed,*" Jackson stated. He then did his best to rouse the Union as a whole:

> Fellow-citizens! the momentous case is before you. On your undivided support of your government depends the decision of the great question it involves, whether your sacred Union will be preserved, and the blessing it secures to us as one people shall be perpetuated. No one can doubt that the unanimity with which that decision will be expressed, will be such as to inspire new confidence in republican institutions, and that the prudence, the wisdom, and the courage which it will bring to their defense, will transmit them unimpaired and invigorated to our children. May the Great Ruler of nations grant that the signal blessings with which he has favored ours may not, by the madness of party, or personal ambition, be disregarded and lost, and may His wise providence bring those who have produced this crisis to see the folly, before they feel the misery, of

civil strife, and inspire a returning veneration for that Union which, if we may dare to penetrate his designs, he has chosen, as the only means of attaining the high destinies to which we may reasonably aspire.

Jackson would bring the full weight of the executive branch's power upon the nullifiers for the sake of the Union.[28] In private, Jackson staked his entire character and reputation on a victory against nullification.

"There can be no nullifier that is not at heart a traitor to our happy constitution, and our union, upon which our own liberty, and that of the whole world rests," Jackson confided to a minister. "If we should fail, and our blessed union be dissolved, the civil wars, blood and destruction must be our unfortunate lot, and despotism will again triumph over the world. But my friend the union shall be preserved, or I perish with it."[29]

In a moment of soul searching, President Jackson corresponded with his old Senate ally, Nathaniel Macon of North Carolina. Macon, along with Randolph, had been a leading Old Republican. Jackson admitted that while he still believed in Thomas Jefferson's and James Madison's Virginia and Kentucky Resolutions of 1798 and 1799, he also believed in the Union. Macon, in response, disagreed with Jackson's decision to challenge nullification, but he recognized Jackson as an honorable man trying to balance two contending principles.

On March 2, 1833, Jackson signed into law what was called the "Force Bill." Written, ironically enough, by Jackson's old enemy, Henry Clay, the bill empowered the executive to force South Carolina's compliance with the tariff laws of the federal government. Armed with the support of Congress, Jackson called up militias, ordered three divisions of artillery to South Carolina, gave General Winfield Scott command over Charleston Harbor, ordered the reinforcement of Charleston's federal forts, and placed naval warships just offshore. With the stick came a carrot—another compromise tariff bill. South Carolina's convention repealed its ordinance of nullification—but, as an act of defiance, nullified Congress's "Force Bill" that had authorized Jackson to take action—and the crisis was over. South Carolina could claim it had forced the amendment of an unjust tariff and stood tall against a threatening federal government, but Jackson knew that he had won—he had preserved the Union.

Chapter Eight

True Republican, True American, and True Heir

I t seems clear that earlier historians who ranked Jackson highly as a president were right. He was surely one of the most consequential and principled presidents in American history. If Jackson has become unfashionable, it is not because we have outgrown his virtues, but because we have need of them.

In late July 1834, Vice President Van Buren thanked and reassured President Jackson that he had, all along, been the right man for the job. In a republic, he claimed, there is always tension "between Aristocracy and Democracy" and that tension must always confront a free people. "It requires constant vigilance to keep the former under anything like subjection. You have done more to cripple its spirit than any, not to say, all your predecessors." As Van Buren pointed out, that many hated Jackson meant he had done well: "Their hatred is the best evidence of your orthodoxy, and the highest compliment that can be paid to your patriotism."[1]

Much like Reagan in the 1980s, Jackson had his ardent followers and supporters. Few remained neutral about either man. And, much like Reagan, Jackson undid the era before him and gave America a new way of seeing things for the generation to come. However poorly we might have squandered the legacy Reagan left for us, he gave us at least twenty years of economic growth and courage in the midst of a chaotic world. The same is true of Jackson, though the issues he faced were different. Martin Van Buren and James K. Polk were ardent disciples of the man, and others, less worthy, such as James Buchanan, claimed to be as well. Had Buchanan reacted in 1860 and 1861 as Jackson did in 1832 and 1833, the entire history of the United States would be different.

Though history has come to associate Jackson with the Democratic Party, the latter really developed under and for Martin Van Buren. Simply put, Jackson thought of himself as a republican and those who challenged him as representatives of the opposition—some well meaning, many not. Informed by Plato's *Laws* and Aristotle's *Politics*, the West had accepted that the best governance includes aristocratic, monarchical, and democratic elements, working in harmony and disharmony. A republic, generally regarded in the West as the best but most fragile government, balances all three. Undoubtedly, Jackson offered America a more charitable view of the average person, the farmer, the worker, and the producer. Though he was certainly a republican, he ardently believed in the democratic element of the three branches of government, prioritizing the will of the people over the aristocratic and monarchical parts. He used the executive office extensively, and, largely through his example, a strong presidency came into existence. Yet, it would take a very long time for the presidency to become permanently strong.

In the nineteenth century, only Lincoln rivaled (and exceeded) Jackson's presidency in terms of strength. It was not until Teddy Roosevelt, Woodrow Wilson, Franklin Roosevelt, and the progressives that the executive branch gained its permanent powers, which have grown outrageously over the previous century. Jackson would never have allowed such proliferation as he never intended to make the executive branch greater or lesser than the legislative or judicial branch; he just wanted it to have an equal say. As John Marshall did with the Supreme Court in *Marbury v. Madison*, Jackson made the president an equal, not a superior.

Jackson was not only the first strong executive in American history, he was also the first, self-made, entrepreneurial frontiersman to hold the office. T. S. Eliot believed America ended with the election of 1828 because neither he nor his New England forbearers could understand Jackson. To them and to many of his own contemporaries, especially those from the northeast and Europe, Jackson was an uncouth, uneducated, Celtic barbarian, informed by a code of honor that should have died at the end of medieval Scotland. That it not only existed in Jackson but also thrived with flair and power upset many people, here and abroad. In this sense, Andrew Jackson, arguably, was the first American president because he was the first executive to cast off traditional, British sensibilities and embrace a thoroughly American persona. He was not an elite, and he was not liberally educated. But he knew the Bible, the Declaration of Independence, the Constitution, and his own experiences on the frontier and in war. That was more than enough to make him an American, a republican, and a great president.

—

Though Americans remember the farewell addresses of Washington and Eisenhower, most have been long forgotten. Sadly, this includes the farewell address of our nation's seventh president. It is time for us to unbox Jackson's "parting" words from the attic of our memories and rediscover the profound wisdom they still offer.

In his final statement as president, Jackson argued that Europe had experienced revolution, upheaval, and war ever since the French Revolution. America, in contrast, had simply attempted to understand and perpetuate a republican constitution, steadfast for the most part but also keenly aware of the imperfections that creep into any form of government. "Our Constitution is no longer a doubtful experiment; and at the end of nearly half a century, we find that it has preserved unimpaired the liberties of the people, secured the rights of property, and that our country has improved and is flourishing beyond any former example in the history of nations."

No matter our domestic or foreign difficulties, he continued, the Union—under the republican constitution—"must be preserved." There will always be those, especially in a republic that nourishes freedom, who desire to tear down the entire edifice. And, though the finest of governments, republics are also the most fragile and prone to dissension and division. "If the Union is once severed, the line of separation will grow wider and wider," Jackson warned. Pride and passion each belong to human nature, and each must exist for it to flourish. But, as with all good things, pride and passion must be tempered by other considerations and only actualized within certain contexts. To let either rule is to move toward ruin.

The very nature of liberty, Jackson warned, contains the seeds of its own destruction and nourishing. To imagine that the constitution can be preserved through force is folly. Only a people freely choosing a republic, freely choosing virtue, and freely choosing to adhere to law can endure. Yet, each republican must be willing to sacrifice himself and his liberty the moment the public good is endangered. "No free government can stand without virtue in the people."

History demonstrates that governments of all types—past and present—love to consolidate power, greedily taking more and more authority from citizens whenever their vigilance against totalitarianism relaxes. There is no need, however, to increase power at any level in the United States. The governments as they now exist, Jackson assured his fellow Americans, can readily address all problems they face. This is especially true for the federal government. "Its legitimate authority is abundantly sufficient for all the purposes for which it was created, and its powers being expressly enumerated, there can be no justification for claiming anything beyond them," Jackson stated. "Every attempt to exercise power beyond these limits should be promptly and firmly opposed, for one evil example will lead to other measures still more mischievous."

If America falls, Jackson believed, it will fall because of taxation, which could destroy the integrity of producers and workers. Because average, hard-working Americans simply work and mind their own business, they often miss the duplicity of words and laws that favor the unproductive, who gain wealth through deceitful and ill-gotten means. This is especially true of corporations, which use laws and tariffs to enrich themselves at the expense of those who actually work. The people, therefore, must be vigilant at all times, protecting themselves from politicians, bureaucrats, and corporations. Should the government stay out of banking and currency, Jackson argued, the average citizen will have less to worry about as there will be fewer opportunities for selfish interests to manipulate.

Jackson went on to explain that evils rarely appear as evils. More often, they disguise themselves attractively and enticingly as friends. No foreign power, he continued, would dare excite us to war. Thus, the real corruption and danger comes, as always in a republic, from within. "It is from within, among yourselves, from cupidity, from corruption, from disappointed ambition, and inordinate thirst for power that factions will be formed and liberty endangered. It is against such designs, whatever disguise the actors may assume, that you have especially to guard yourselves." For reasons beyond our ken, God has chosen this soil and those born to it to be the inheritors of liberty. This is as much a divine burden as it is a divine gift. "May He who holds in His hands the destinies of nations make you worthy of the favors He has bestowed and enable you, with pure hearts and pure hands and sleepless vigilance, to guard and defend to the end of time the great charge He has committed to your keeping."

As Jackson's biography so amply reveals, the closing remarks of his farewell address were not mere words to him. They were manifestations of his soul, which is reflected in the way he lived. However violent or angry he became, Jackson always returned to actions and words of honor. Even at the end of his life, long after the glories of war and the presidency had faded, he maintained his principles. When supporters offered to build a mausoleum to his memory after his death, he declined. Though he was deeply honored at being recognized for whatever excellences he may have achieved, he stated, "my republican feelings and principles forbid it; the simplicity of our system of Government forbids it." Republican virtue is demonstrated only in simplicity and directness. "True virtue cannot exist where pomp and parade are the governing passions; it can only dwell with the people, the great laboring and producing classes, that form the bone and sinew of our Confederacy."[2]

In an America that builds the most massive shrines to the power of the corrupt and the manipulative—such as the Franklin D. Roosevelt or Lyndon B. Johnson presidential libraries—Jackson seems more than a world away from us. But continuing to study his enduring legacy will help us grasp at the noble principles that inspired the man who devoted his life to making democracy possible and the Union inviolable.

Jackson was a true republican, a true American, and a true heir to the founding fathers. In an age that wants to disparage and forget the past, we would do well to re-engage with it and remind ourselves of the principles and controversies and debates that undergird the great American experiment in republican government. Without that memory, our republic will not long endure.

Appendix

President Andrew Jackson's Farewell Address, March 4, 1837

FELLOW-CITIZENS: Being about to retire finally from public life, I beg leave to offer you my grateful thanks for the many proofs of kindness and confidence which I have received at your hands. It has been my fortune in the discharge of public duties, civil and military, frequently to have found myself in difficult and trying situations, where prompt decision and energetic action were necessary, and where the interest of the country required that high responsibilities should be fearlessly encountered; and it is with the deepest emotions of gratitude that I acknowledge the continued and unbroken confidence with which you have sustained me in every trial. My public life has been a long one, and I can not hope that it has at all times been free from errors; but I have the consolation of knowing that if mistakes have been committed they have not seriously injured the country I so anxiously endeavored to serve, and at the moment when I surrender my last public trust I leave this great people prosperous and happy, in the full enjoyment of liberty and peace, and honored and respected by every nation of the world.

If my humble efforts have in any degree contributed to preserve to you these blessings, I have been more than rewarded by the honors you have heaped upon me, and, above all, by the generous confidence with which you have supported me in every peril, and with which you have continued to animate and cheer my path to the closing hour of my political life. The time has now come when advanced age and a broken frame warn me to retire from public concerns, but the recollection of the many favors you have bestowed upon me is engraven upon my heart, and I have felt that I could not part from your service without making this public acknowledgment of the gratitude I owe you. And if I use the occasion to offer to you the counsels of age and experience, you will, I trust, receive them with the same indulgent kindness which you have so often extended to me, and will at least see in them an earnest desire to perpetuate in this favored land the blessings of liberty and equal law.

We have now lived almost fifty years under the Constitution framed by the sages and patriots of the Revolution. The conflicts in which the nations of Europe were engaged during a great part of this period, the spirit in which they waged war against each other, and our intimate commercial connections with every part of the civilized world rendered it a time of much difficulty for the Government of the United States. We have had our seasons of peace and of war, with all the evils which precede or follow a state of hostility with powerful nations. We encountered these trials with our Constitution yet in its infancy, and under the disadvantages which a new and untried government must always feel when it is called upon to put forth its whole strength without the lights of experience to guide it or the weight of precedents to justify its measures. But we have passed triumphantly through all these difficulties. Our Constitution is no longer a doubtful experiment, and at the end of nearly half a century we find that it has preserved unimpaired the liberties of the people, secured the rights of property, and that our country has improved and is flourishing beyond any former example in the history of nations.

In our domestic concerns there is everything to encourage us, and if you are true to yourselves nothing can impede your march to the highest point of national prosperity. The States which had so long been retarded in their improvement by the Indian tribes residing in the midst of them are at length relieved from the evil, and this unhappy race—the original dwellers in our land—are now placed in a situation where we may well hope that they will share in the blessings of civilization and be saved from that degradation and destruction to which they were rapidly hastening while they remained in the States; and while the safety and comfort of our own citizens have been greatly promoted by their removal, the philanthropist will rejoice that the remnant of that ill-fated race has been at length placed beyond the reach of injury or oppression, and that the paternal care of the General Government will hereafter watch over them and protect them.

If we turn to our relations with foreign powers, we find our condition equally gratifying. Actuated by the sincere desire to do justice to every nation and to preserve the blessings of peace, our intercourse with them has been conducted on the part of this Government in the spirit of frankness; and I take pleasure in saying that it has generally been met in a corresponding temper. Difficulties of old standing have been surmounted by friendly discussion and the mutual desire to be just, and the claims of our citizens, which had been long withheld, have at length been acknowledged and adjusted and satisfactory arrangements made for their final payment; and with a limited, and I trust a temporary, exception, our relations with every foreign power are now of the most friendly character, our commerce continually expanding, and our flag respected in every quarter of the world.

These cheering and grateful prospects and these multiplied favors we owe, under Providence, to the adoption of the Federal Constitution. It is no longer a question whether this great country can remain happily united and flourish under our present form of government. Experience, the unerring test of all human undertakings, has shown the wisdom and foresight of those who formed it, and has proved that in the union of these States there is a sure foundation for the brightest hopes of freedom and for the happiness of the people. At every hazard and by every sacrifice this Union must be preserved.

The necessity of watching with jealous anxiety for the preservation of the Union was earnestly pressed upon his fellow-citizens by the Father of his Country in his Farewell Address. He has there told us that "while experience shall not have demonstrated its impracticability, there will always be reason to distrust the patriotism of those who in any quarter may endeavor to weaken its bands;" and he has cautioned us in the strongest terms against the formation of parties on geographical discriminations, as one of the means which might disturb our Union and to which designing men would be likely to resort.

The lessons contained in this invaluable legacy of Washington to his countrymen should be cherished in the heart of every citizen to the latest generation; and perhaps at no period of time could they be more usefully remembered than at the present moment; for when we look upon the scenes that are passing around us and dwell upon the pages of his parting address, his paternal counsels would seem to be not merely the offspring of wisdom and foresight, but the voice of prophecy, foretelling events and warning us of the evil to come. Forty years have passed since this imperishable document was given to his countrymen. The Federal Constitution was then regarded by him as an experiment—and he so speaks of it in his Address—but an experiment upon the success of which the best hopes of his country depended; and we all know that he was prepared to lay down his life, if necessary, to secure to it a full and a fair trial. The trial has been made. It has succeeded beyond the proudest hopes of those who framed it. Every quarter of this widely extended nation has felt its blessings and shared in the general prosperity produced by its adoption. But amid this general prosperity and splendid success the dangers of which he warned us are becoming every day more evident, and the signs of evil are sufficiently apparent to awaken the deepest anxiety in the bosom of the patriot. We behold systematic efforts publicly made to sow the seeds of discord between different parts of the United States and to place party divisions directly upon geographical distinctions; to excite the *South* against the *North* and the *North* against the *South* , and to force into the controversy the most delicate and exciting topics—topics upon which it is impossible that a large portion of the Union can ever speak without strong emotion. Appeals, too, are constantly made to sectional interests in order to influence the election of the Chief Magistrate, as if it were desired that he should favor a particular quarter of the country instead of fulfilling the duties of his station with impartial justice to all; and the possible dissolution of the Union has at length become an ordinary and familiar subject of discussion. Has the warning voice of Washington been forgotten, or have designs already been formed to sever the Union? Let it not be supposed that I impute to all of those who have taken an active part in these unwise and unprofitable discussions a want of patriotism or of public virtue. The honorable feeling of State pride and local attachments finds a place in the bosoms of the most enlightened and pure. But while such men are conscious of their own integrity and honesty of purpose, they ought never to forget that the citizens of other States are their political brethren, and that however mistaken they may be in their views, the great body of them are equally honest and upright with themselves. Mutual suspicions and reproaches may in time create mutual hostility, and artful and designing men will always be found who are ready to foment these fatal divisions and to inflame the natural jealousies of different sections of the country. The history of the world is full of such examples, and especially the history of republics.

What have you to gain by division and dissension? Delude not yourselves with the belief that a breach once made may be afterwards repaired. If the Union is once severed, the line of separation will grow wider and wider, and the controversies which are now debated and settled in the halls of legislation will then be tried in fields of battle and determined by the sword. Neither should you deceive yourselves with the hope that the first line of separation would be the permanent one, and that nothing but harmony and concord would be found in the new associations formed upon the dissolution of this Union. Local interests would still be found there, and unchastened ambition. And if the recollection of common dangers, in which the people of these United States stood side by side against the common foe, the memory of victories won by their united valor, the prosperity and happiness they have enjoyed under the present Constitution, the proud name they bear as citizens of this great Republic—if all these recollections and proofs of common interest are not strong enough to bind us together as one people, what tie will hold united the new divisions of empire when these bonds have been broken and this Union dissevered ? The first line of separation would not last for a single generation; new fragments would be torn off, new leaders would spring up, and this great and glorious Republic would soon be broken into a multitude of petty States, without commerce, without credit, jealous of one another, armed for mutual aggression, loaded with taxes to pay armies and leaders, seeking aid against each other from foreign powers, insulted and trampled upon by the nations of Europe, until, harassed with conflicts and humbled and debased in spirit, they would be ready to submit to the absolute dominion of any military adventurer and to surrender their liberty for the sake of repose. It is impossible to look on the consequences that would inevitably follow the destruction of this Government and not feel indignant when we hear cold calculations about the value of the Union and have so constantly before us a line of conduct so well calculated to weaken its ties.

There is too much at stake to allow pride or passion to influence your decision. Never for a moment believe that the great body of the citizens of any State or States can deliberately intend to do wrong. They may, under the influence of temporary excitement or misguided opinions, commit mistakes; they may be misled for a time by the suggestions of self-interest; but in a community so enlightened and patriotic as the people of the United States argument will soon make them sensible of their errors, and when convinced they will be ready to repair them. If they have no higher or better motives to govern them, they will at least perceive that their own interest requires them to be just to others, as they hope to receive justice at their hands.

But in order to maintain the Union unimpaired it is absolutely necessary that the laws passed by the constituted authorities should be faithfully executed in every part of the country, and that every good citizen should at all times stand ready to put down, with the combined force of the nation, every attempt at unlawful resistance, under whatever pretext it may be made or whatever shape it may assume. Unconstitutional or oppressive laws may no doubt be passed by Congress, either from erroneous views or the want of due consideration; if they are within the reach of judicial authority, the remedy is easy and peaceful; and if, from the character of the law, it is an abuse of power not within the control of the judiciary, then free discussion and calm appeals to reason and to the justice of the people will not fail to redress the wrong. But until the law shall be declared void by the courts or repealed by Congress no individual or combination of individuals can be justified in forcibly resisting its execution. It is impossible that any government can continue to exist upon any other principles. It would cease to be a government and be unworthy of the name if it had not the power to enforce the execution of its own laws within its own sphere of action.

It is true that cases may be imagined disclosing such a settled purpose of usurpation and oppression on the part of the Government as would justify an appeal to arms. These, however, are extreme cases, which we have no reason to apprehend in a government where the power is in the hands of a patriotic people. And no citizen who loves his country would in any case whatever resort to forcible resistance unless he clearly saw that the time had come when a freeman should prefer death to submission; for if such a struggle is once begun, and the citizens of one section of the country arrayed in arms against those of another in doubtful conflict, let the battle result as it may, there will be an end of the Union and with it an end to the hopes of freedom. The victory of the injured would not secure to them the blessings of liberty; it would avenge their wrongs, but they would themselves share in the common ruin.

But the Constitution can not be maintained nor the Union preserved, in opposition to public feeling, by the mere exertion of the coercive powers confided to the General Government. The foundations must be laid in the affections of the people, in the security it gives to life, liberty, character, and property in every quarter of the country, and in the fraternal attachment which the citizens of the several States bear to one another as members of one political family, mutually contributing to promote the happiness of each other. Hence the citizens of every State should studiously avoid everything calculated to wound the sensibility or offend the just pride of the people of other States, and they should frown upon any proceedings within their own borders likely to disturb the tranquillity of their political brethren in other portions of the Union. In a country so extensive as the United States, and with pursuits so varied, the internal regulations of the several States must frequently differ from one another in important particulars, and this difference is unavoidably increased by the varying principles upon which the American colonies were originally planted—principles which had taken deep root in their social relations before the Revolution, and therefore of necessity influencing their policy since they became free and independent States. But each State has the unquestionable right to regulate its own internal concerns according to its own pleasure, and while it does not interfere with the rights of the people of other States or the rights of the Union, every State must be the sole judge of the measures proper to secure the safety of its citizens and promote their happiness; and all efforts on the part of people of other States to cast odium upon their institutions, and all measures calculated to disturb their rights of property or to put in jeopardy their peace and internal tranquillity, are in direct opposition to the spirit in which the Union was formed, and must endanger its safety. Motives of philanthropy may be assigned for this unwarrantable interference, and weak men may persuade themselves for a moment that they are laboring in the cause of humanity and asserting the rights of the human race; but everyone, upon sober reflection, will see that nothing but mischief can come from these improper assaults upon the feelings and rights of others. Rest assured that the men found busy in this work of discord are not worthy of your confidence, and deserve your strongest reprobation.

In the legislation of Congress also, and in every measure of the General Government, justice to every portion of the United States should be faithfully observed. No free government can stand without virtue in the people and a lofty spirit of patriotism, and if the sordid feelings of mere selfishness shall usurp the place which ought to be filled by public spirit, the legislation of Congress will soon be converted into a scramble for personal and sectional advantages. Under our free institutions the citizens of every quarter of our country are capable of attaining a high degree of prosperity and happiness without seeking to profit themselves at the expense of others; and every such attempt must in the end fail to succeed, for the people in every part of the United States are too enlightened not to understand their own rights and interests and to detect and defeat every effort to gain undue advantages over them; and when such designs are discovered it naturally provokes resentments which can not always be easily allayed. Justice—full and ample justice to every portion of the United States should be the ruling principle of every freeman, and should guide the deliberations of every public body, whether it be State or national.

It is well known that there have always been those amongst us who wish to enlarge the powers of the. General Government, and experience would seem to indicate that there is a tendency on the part of this Government to overstep the boundaries marked out for it by the Constitution. Its legitimate authority is abundantly sufficient for all the purposes for which it was created, and its powers being expressly enumerated, there can be no justification for claiming anything beyond them. Every attempt to exercise power beyond these limits should be promptly and firmly opposed, for one evil example will lead to other measures still more mischievous; and if the principle of constructive powers or supposed advantages or temporary circumstances shall ever be permitted to justify the assumption of a power not given by the Constitution, the General Government will before long absorb all the powers of legislation, and you will have in effect but one consolidated government. From the extent of our country, its diversified interests, different pursuits, and different habits, it is too obvious for argument that a single consolidated government would be wholly inadequate to watch over and protect its interests; and every friend of our free institutions should be always prepared to maintain unimpaired and in full vigor the rights and sovereignty of the States and to confine the action of the General Government strictly to the sphere of its appropriate duties.

There is, perhaps, no one of the powers conferred on the Federal Government so liable to abuse as the taxing power. The most productive and convenient sources of revenue were necessarily given to it, that it might be able to perform the important duties imposed upon it; and the taxes which it lays upon commerce being concealed from the real payer in the price of the article, they do not so readily attract the attention of the people as smaller sums demanded from them directly by the taxgatherer. But the tax imposed on goods enhances by so much the price of the commodity to the consumer, and as many of these duties are imposed on articles of necessity which are daily used by the great body of the people, the money raised by these imposts is drawn from their pockets. Congress has no right under the Constitution to take money from the people unless it is required to execute some one of the specific powers intrusted to the Government; and if they raise more than is necessary for such purposes, it is an abuse of the power of taxation, and unjust and oppressive. It may indeed happen that the revenue will sometimes exceed the amount anticipated when the taxes were laid. When, however, this is ascertained, it is easy to reduce them, and in such a case it is unquestionably the duty of the Government to reduce them, for no circumstances can justify it in assuming a power not given to it by the Constitution nor in taking away the money of the people when it is not needed for the legitimate wants of the Government.

Plain as these principles appear to be, you will yet find there is a constant effort to induce the General Government to go beyond the limits of its taxing power and to impose unnecessary burdens upon the people. Many powerful interests are continually at work to procure heavy duties on commerce and to swell the revenue beyond the real necessities of the public service, and the country has already felt the injurious effects of their combined influence. They succeeded in obtaining a tariff of duties bearing most oppressively on the agricultural and laboring classes of society and producing a revenue that could not be usefully employed within the range of the powers conferred upon

Congress, and in order to fasten upon the people this unjust and unequal system of taxation extravagant schemes of internal improvement were got up in various quarters to squander the money and to purchase support. Thus one unconstitutional measure was intended to be upheld by another, and the abuse of the power of taxation was to be maintained by usurping the power of expending the money in internal improvements. You can not have forgotten the severe and doubtful struggle through which we passed when the executive department of the Government by its veto endeavored to arrest this prodigal scheme of injustice and to bring back the legislation of Congress to the boundaries prescribed by the Constitution. The good sense and practical judgment of the people when the subject was brought before them sustained the course of the Executive, and this plan of unconstitutional expenditures for the purposes of corrupt influence is, I trust, finally overthrown.

The result of this decision has been felt in the rapid extinguishment of the public debt and the large accumulation of a surplus in the Treasury, notwithstanding the tariff was reduced and is now very far below the amount originally contemplated by its advocates. But, rely upon it, the design to collect an extravagant revenue and to burden you with taxes beyond the economical wants of the Government is not yet abandoned. The various interests which have combined together to impose a heavy tariff and to produce an overflowing Treasury are too strong and have too much at stake to surrender the contest. The corporations and wealthy individuals who are engaged in large manufacturing establishments desire a high tariff to increase their gains. Designing politicians will support it to conciliate their favor and to obtain the means of profuse expenditure for the purpose of purchasing influence in other quarters; and since the people have decided that the Federal Government can not be permitted to employ its income in internal improvements, efforts will be made to seduce and mislead the citizens of the several States by holding out to them the deceitful prospect of benefits to be derived from a surplus revenue collected by the General Government and annually divided among the States; and if, encouraged by these fallacious hopes, the States should disregard the principles of economy which ought to characterize every republican government, and should indulge in lavish expenditures exceeding their resources, they will before long find themselves oppressed with debts which they are unable to pay, and the temptation will become irresistible to support a high tariff in order to obtain a surplus for distribution. Do not allow yourselves, my fellow-citizens, to be misled on this subject. The Federal Government can not collect a surplus for such purposes without violating the principles of the Constitution and assuming powers which have not been granted. It is, moreover, a system of injustice, and if persisted in will inevitably lead to corruption, and must end in ruin. The surplus revenue will be drawn from the pockets of the people—from the farmer, the mechanic, and the laboring classes of society; but who will receive it when distributed among the States, where it is to be disposed of by leading State politicians, who have friends to favor and political partisans to gratify ? It will certainly not be returned to those who paid it and who have most need of it and are honestly entitled to it. There is but one safe rule, and that is to confine the General Government rigidly within the sphere of its appropriate duties. It has no power to raise a revenue or impose taxes except for the purposes enumerated in the Constitution, and if its income is found to exceed these wants it should be forthwith reduced and the burden of the people so far lightened.

In reviewing the conflicts which have taken place between different interests in the United States and the policy pursued since the adoption of our present form of Government, we find nothing that has produced such deep-seated evil as the course of legislation in relation to the currency. The Constitution of the United States unquestionably intended to secure to the people a circulating medium of gold and silver. But the establishment of a national bank by Congress, with the privilege of issuing paper money receivable in the payment of the public dues, and the unfortunate course of legislation in the several States upon the same subject, drove from general circulation the constitutional currency and substituted one of paper in its place.

It was not easy for men engaged in the ordinary pursuits of business, whose attention had not been particularly drawn to the subject, to foresee all the consequences of a currency exclusively of paper, and we ought not on that account to be surprised at the facility with which laws were obtained to carry into effect the paper system. Honest and even enlightened men are sometimes misled by the specious and plausible statements of the designing. But experience has now proved the mischiefs and dangers of a paper currency, and it rests with you to determine whether the proper remedy shall be applied.

The paper system being founded on public confidence and having of itself no intrinsic value, it is liable to great and sudden fluctuations, thereby rendering property insecure and the wages of labor unsteady and uncertain. The corporations which create the paper money can not be relied upon to keep the circulating medium uniform in amount. In times of prosperity, when confidence is high, they are tempted by the prospect of gain or by the influence of those who hope to profit by it to extend their issues of paper beyond the bounds of discretion and the reasonable demands of business; and when these issues have been pushed on from day to day, until public confidence is at length shaken, then a reaction takes place, and they immediately withdraw the credits they have given, suddenly curtail their issues, and produce an unexpected and ruinous contraction of the circulating medium, which is felt by the whole community. The banks by this means save themselves, and the mischievous consequences of their imprudence or cupidity are visited upon the public. Nor does the evil stop here. These ebbs and flows in the currency and these indiscreet extensions of credit naturally engender a spirit of speculation injurious to the habits and character of the people. We have already seen its effects in the wild spirit of speculation in the public lands and various kinds of stock which within the last year or two seized upon such a multitude of our citizens and threatened to pervade all classes of society and to withdraw their attention from the sober pursuits of honest industry. It is not by encouraging this spirit that we shall best preserve public virtue and promote the true interests of our country; but if your currency continues as exclusively paper as it now is, it will foster this eager desire to amass wealth without labor; it will multiply the number of dependents on bank accommodations and bank favors; the temptation to obtain money at any sacrifice will become stronger and stronger, and inevitably lead to corruption, which will find its way into your public councils and destroy at no distant day the purity of your Government. Some of the evils which arise from this system of paper press with peculiar hardship upon the class of society least able to bear it. A portion of this currency frequently becomes depreciated or worthless, and all of it is easily counterfeited in such a manner as to require peculiar skill and much experience to distinguish the counterfeit from the genuine note. These frauds are most generally perpetrated in the smaller notes, which are used in the daily transactions of ordinary business, and the losses occasioned by them are commonly thrown upon the laboring classes of society, whose situation and pursuits put it out of their power to guard themselves from these impositions, and whose daily wages are necessary for their subsistence. It is the duty of every government so to regulate its currency as to protect this numerous class, as far as practicable, from the impositions of avarice and fraud. It is more especially the duty of the United States, where the Government is emphatically the Government of the people, and where this respectable portion of our citizens are so proudly distinguished from the laboring classes of all other nations by their independent spirit, their love of liberty, their intelligence, and their high tone of moral character. Their industry in peace is the source of our wealth and their bravery in war has covered us with glory; and the Government of the United States will but ill discharge its duties if it leaves them a prey to such dishonest impositions. Yet it is evident that their interests can not be effectually protected unless silver and gold are restored to circulation.

These views alone of the paper currency are sufficient to call for immediate reform; but there is another consideration which should still more strongly press it upon your attention.

Recent events have proved that the paper-money system of this country may be used as an engine to undermine your free institutions, and that those who desire to engross all power in the hands of the few and to govern by corruption or force are aware of its power and prepared to employ it. Your banks now furnish your only circulating medium, and money is plenty or scarce according to the quantity of notes issued by them. While they have capitals not greatly disproportioned to each other, they are competitors in business, and no one of them can exercise dominion over the rest; and although in the present state of the currency these banks may and do operate injuriously upon the habits of business, the pecuniary concerns, and the moral tone of society, yet, from their number and dispersed situation, they can not combine for the purposes of political influence, and whatever may be the dispositions of some of them their power of mischief must necessarily be confined to a narrow space and felt only in their immediate neighborhoods.

But when the charter for the Bank of the United States was obtained from Congress it perfected the schemes of the paper system and gave to its advocates the position they have struggled to obtain from the commencement of the Federal Government to the present hour. The immense capital and peculiar privileges bestowed upon it enabled it to exercise despotic sway over the other banks in every part of the country. From its superior strength it could seriously injure, if not destroy, the business of any one of them which might incur its resentment; and it openly claimed for itself the power of regulating the currency throughout the United States. In other words, it asserted (and it undoubtedly possessed) the power to make money plenty or scarce at its pleasure, at any time and in any quarter of the Union, by controlling the issues of other banks and permitting an expansion or compelling a general contraction of the circulating medium, according to its own will. The other banking institutions were sensible of its strength, and they soon generally became its obedient instruments, ready at all times to execute its mandates; and with the banks necessarily went also that numerous class of persons in our commercial cities who depend altogether on bank credits for their solvency and means of business, and who are therefore obliged, for their own safety, to propitiate the favor of the money power by distinguished zeal and devotion in its service. The result of the ill-advised legislation which established this great monopoly was to concentrate the whole moneyed power of the Union, with its boundless means of corruption and its numerous dependents, under the direction and command of one acknowledged head, thus organizing this particular interest as one body and securing to it unity and concert of action throughout the United States, and enabling it to bring forward upon any occasion its entire and undivided strength to support or defeat any measure of the Government. In the hands of this formidable power, thus perfectly organized, was also placed unlimited dominion over the amount of the circulating medium, giving it the power to regulate the value of property and the fruits of labor in every quarter of the Union, and to bestow prosperity or bring ruin upon any city or section of the country as might best comport with its own interest or policy.

We are not left to conjecture how the moneyed power, thus organized and with such a weapon in its hands, would be likely to use it. The distress and alarm which pervaded and agitated the whole country when the Bank of the United States waged war upon the people in order to compel them to submit to its demands can not yet be forgotten. The ruthless and unsparing temper with which whole cities and communities were oppressed, individuals impoverished and ruined, and a scene of cheerful prosperity suddenly changed into one of gloom and despondency ought to be indelibly impressed on the memory of the people of the United States. If such was its power in a time of peace, what would it not have been in a season of war, with an enemy at your doors? No nation but the freemen of the United States could have come out victorious from such a contest; yet, if you had not conquered, the Government would have passed from the hands of the many to the hands of the few, and this organized money power from its secret conclave would have dictated the choice of your highest officers and compelled you to make peace or war, as best suited their own wishes. The forms of your Government might for a time have remained, but its living spirit would have departed from it.

The distress and sufferings inflicted on the people by the bank are some of the fruits of that system of policy which is continually striving to enlarge the authority of the Federal Government beyond the limits fixed by the Constitution. The powers enumerated in that instrument do not confer on Congress the right to establish such a corporation as the Bank of the United States, and the evil consequences which followed may warn us of the danger of departing from the true rule of construction and of permitting temporary circumstances or the hope of better promoting the public welfare to influence in any degree our decisions upon the extent of the authority of the General Government. Let us abide by the Constitution as it is written, or amend it in the constitutional mode if it is found to be defective.

The severe lessons of experience will, I doubt not, be sufficient to prevent Congress from again chartering such a monopoly, even if the Constitution did not present an insuperable objection to it. But you must remember, my fellow-citizens, that eternal vigilance by the people is the price of liberty, and that you must pay the price if you wish to secure the blessing. It behooves you, therefore, to be watchful in your States as well as in the Federal Government. The power which the moneyed interest can exercise, when concentrated under a single head and with our present system of currency, was sufficiently demonstrated in the struggle made by the Bank of the United States. Defeated in the General Government, tho same class of intriguers and politicians will now resort to the States and endeavor to obtain there the same organization which they failed to perpetuate in the Union; and with specious and deceitful plans of public advantages and State interests and State pride they will endeavor to establish in the different States one moneyed institution with overgrown capital and exclusive privileges sufficient to enable it to control the operations of the other banks. Such an institution will be pregnant with the same evils produced by the Bank of the United States, although its sphere of action is more confined, and in the State in which it is chartered the money power will be able to embody its whole strength and to move together with undivided force to accomplish any object it may wish to attain. You have already had abundant evidence of its power to inflict injury upon the agricultural, mechanical, and laboring classes of society, and over those whose engagements in trade or speculation render them dependent on bank facilities the dominion of the State monopoly will be absolute and their obedience unlimited. With such a bank and a paper currency the money power would in a few years govern the State and control its measures, and if a sufficient number of

States can be induced to create such establishments the time will soon come when it will again take the field against the United States and succeed in perfecting and perpetuating its organization by a charter from Congress.

It is one of the serious evils of our present system of banking that it enables one class of society—and that by no means a numerous one—by its control over the currency, to act injuriously upon the interests of all the others and to exercise more than its just proportion of influence in political affairs. The agricultural, the mechanical, and the laboring classes have little or no share in the direction of the great moneyed corporations, and from their habits and the nature of their pursuits they are incapable of forming extensive combinations to act together with united force. Such concert of action may sometimes be produced in a single city or in a small district of country by means of personal communications with each other, but they have no regular or active correspondence with those who are engaged in similar pursuits in distant places; they have but little patronage to give to the press, and exercise but a small share of influence over it; they have no crowd of dependents about them who hope to grow rich without labor by their countenance and favor, and who are therefore always ready to execute their wishes. The planter, the farmer, the mechanic, and the laborer all know that their success depends upon their own industry and economy, and that they must not expect to become suddenly rich by the fruits of their toil. Yet these classes of society form the great body of the people of the United

States; they are the bone and sinew of the country—men who love liberty and desire nothing but equal rights and equal laws, and who, moreover, hold the great mass of our national wealth, although it is distributed in moderate amounts among the millions of freemen who possess it. But with overwhelming numbers and wealth on their side they are in constant danger of losing their fair influence in the Government, and with difficulty maintain their just rights against the incessant efforts daily made to encroach upon them. The mischief springs from the power which the moneyed interest derives from a paper currency which they are able to control, from the multitude of corporations with exclusive privileges which they have succeeded in obtaining in the different States, and which are employed altogether for their benefit; and unless you become more watchful in your States and check this spirit of monopoly and thirst for exclusive privileges you will in the end find that the most important powers of Government have been given or bartered away, and the control over your dearest interests has passed into the hands of these corporations.

The paper-money system and its natural associations—monopoly and exclusive privileges—have already struck their roots too deep in the soil, and it will require all your efforts to check its further growth and to eradicate the evil. The men who profit by the abuses and desire to perpetuate them will continue to besiege the halls of legislation in the General Government as well as in the States, and will seek by every artifice to mislead and deceive the public servants. It is to yourselves that you must look for safety and the means of guarding and perpetuating your free institutions. In your hands is rightfully placed the sovereignty of the country, and to you everyone placed in authority is ultimately responsible. It is always in your power to see that the wishes of the people are carried into faithful execution, and their will, when once made known, must sooner or later be obeyed; and while the people remain, as I trust they ever will, uncorrupted and incorruptible, and continue watchful and jealous of their rights, the Government is safe, and the cause of freedom will continue to triumph over all its enemies.

But it will require steady and persevering exertions on your part to rid yourselves of the iniquities and mischiefs of the paper system and to check the spirit of monopoly and other abuses which have sprung up with it, and of which it is the main support. So many interests are united to resist all reform on this subject that you must not hope the conflict will be a short one nor success easy. My humble efforts have not been spared during my administration of the Government to restore the constitutional currency of gold and silver, and something, I trust, has been done toward the accomplishment of this most desirable object; but enough yet remains to require all your energy and perseverance. The power, however, is in your hands, and the remedy must and will be applied if you determine upon it.

While I am thus endeavoring to press upon your attention the principles which I deem of vital importance in the domestic concerns of the country, I ought not to pass over without notice the important considerations which should govern your policy toward foreign powers. It is unquestionably our true interest to cultivate the most friendly understanding with every nation and to avoid by every honorable means the calamities of war, and we shall best attain this object by frankness and sincerity in our foreign intercourse, by the prompt and faithful execution of treaties, and by justice and impartiality in our conduct to all. But no nation, however desirous of peace, can hope to escape occasional collisions with other powers, and the soundest dictates of policy require that we should place ourselves in a condition to assert our rights if a resort to force should ever become necessary. Our local situation, our long line of seacoast, indented by numerous bays, with deep rivers opening into the interior, as well as our extended and still increasing commerce, point to the Navy as our natural means of defense. It will in the end be found to be the cheapest and most effectual, and now is the time, in a season of peace and with an overflowing revenue, that we can year after year add to its strength without increasing the burdens of the people. It is your true policy, for your Navy will not only protect your rich and flourishing commerce in distant seas, but will enable you to reach and annoy the enemy and will give to defense its greatest efficiency by meeting danger at a distance from home. It is impossible by any line of fortifications to guard every point from attack against a hostile force advancing from the ocean and selecting its object, but they are indispensable to protect cities from bombardment, dockyards and naval arsenals from destruction, to give shelter to merchant vessels in time of war and to single ships or weaker squadrons when pressed by superior force. Fortifications of this description can not be too soon completed and armed and placed in a condition of the most perfect preparation. The abundant means we now possess can not be applied in any manner more useful to the country, and when this is done and our naval force sufficiently strengthened and our militia armed we need not fear that any nation will wantonly insult us or needlessly provoke hostilities. We shall more certainly preserve peace when it is well understood that we are prepared for War.

In presenting to you, my fellow-citizens, these parting counsels, I have brought before you the leading principles upon which I endeavored to administer the Government in the high office with which you twice honored me. Knowing that the path of freedom is continually beset by enemies who often assume the disguise of friends, I have devoted the last hours of my public life to warn you of the dangers. The progress of the United States under our free and happy institutions has surpassed the most sanguine hopes of the founders of the Republic. Our growth has been rapid beyond all former example in numbers, in wealth, in knowledge, and all the useful arts which contribute to the comforts and convenience of man, and from the earliest ages of history to the present day there never have been thirteen millions of people associated in one political body who enjoyed so much freedom and happiness as the people of these United States. You have no longer any cause to fear danger from abroad; your strength and power are well known throughout the civilized world, as well as the high and gallant bearing of your sons. It is from within, among your-selves—from cupidity, from corruption, from disappointed ambi-tion and inordinate thirst for power—that factions will be formed and liberty endangered. It is against such designs, whatever dis-guise the actors may assume, that you have especially to guard yourselves. You have the highest of human trusts committed to your care. Providence has showered on this favored land blessings without number, and has chosen you as the guardians of freedom, to preserve it for the benefit of the human race. May He who holds in His hands the destinies of nations make you worthy of the favors He has bestowed and enable you, with pure hearts and pure hands and sleepless vigilance, to guard and defend to the end of time the great charge He has committed to your keeping.

My own race is nearly run; advanced age and failing health warn me that before long I must pass beyond the reach of human events and cease to feel the vicissitudes of human affairs. I thank God that my life has been spent in a land of liberty and that He has given me a heart to love my country with the affection of a son. And filled with gratitude for your constant and unwavering kindness, I bid you a last and affectionate farewell.

ANDREW JACKSON.

Notes

Chapter One: Andrew Jackson and His Meaning to America

1. Margaret Bayard, *The First Forty Years of Washington Society* (New York: Charles Scribner's Sons, 1906), 292, 293.

2. Arthur J. Stansbury, quoted in Parton, *The Life of Andrew Jackson* 3: 169.

3. Bayard, *The First Forty Years of Washington Society*, 292, 293.

4. Bayard, *The First Forty Years*, 292; and Joseph Story to his wife, March 7, 1829, in *Life and Letters of Joseph Story*, ed. by William W. Story, Vol 1 (Boston MA: Little and Brown, 1851), 562-563.

5. Bayard, *The First Forty Years*, 292.

6. Senator Hamilton to Martin Van Buren, March 5, 1829, in the Martin Van Buren Papers, Library of Congress. Photostat available online through the LOC.

7. As described later in this book, Jackson loved his wife to such an extent that he considered her, along with his mother, sainted. See, for example, his description of her tomb as a shrine: AJ to Manuel J. Hays, April 19, 1830, in Dorsey D. Jones, ed., "A Jackson Letter," *Journal of Southern History* 20 (February 1954): 91-92.

8. James Parton, *The Life of Andrew Jackson*, Vol. 3 (New York: Mason, 1860), 164-166.

9. "The Inauguration," reprinted from the *United States Telegraph* in *Louisville Public Advertiser* (March 21, 1829).

10. "The Inauguration," reprinted from the *United States Telegraph* in *Louisville Public Advertiser* (March 21, 1829).

11. Bayard, *The First Forty Years*, 291.

12. John Adams, quoted in *Major Problems of the Early Republic*, 20.

13. "The Inauguration," reprinted from the *United States Telegraph* in *Louisville Public Advertiser* (March 21, 1829).

14. Bayard, *The First Forty Years*, 293.

15. One of Jackson's most important biographers, Robert Remini, details the immense corruption of the so-called Era of Good Feelings in the Monroe and J.Q. Adams administrations, in his various works on Jackson. He does not condemn either of Jackson's presidential predecessors, but he notes that the prevailing attitude in D.C. during the previous two administrations was one of taking what one could, especially at the moral and economic expense of the American taxpayer. See, for instance, Remini's chapter 14, "The Reform Begins," in *The Life of Andrew Jackson* (American Political Biography Press, 2003).

16. Andrew Jackson, "Inaugural Address," *Raleigh Register and North Carolina Gazette* (March 10, 1829.

17. Bayard, *The First Forty Years*, 290.

18. Bayard, *The First Forty Years*, 295.

19. Stansbury, quoted in Parton, *Life of Andrew Jackson* 3: 169.

20. Story to his wife, March 7, 1829, in *Life and Letters of Joseph Story* 1: 563.

21. Parton, *Life of Andrew Jackson* 3: 170-171.

22. Walter Nugent, *Structures of American Social History* (The Hebrew University Magnes Press, 1981), 54-55, 57.

23. Tocqueville, *Democracy in America*, 882.

24. Malcolm J. Rohrbough, *The Trans-Appalachian Frontier*, (Indiana University Press, 2008), 158.

25. The Jacksons adopted three sons—Andrew Jackson Jr., who was actually the son of Rachel's brother Severn Donelson, and two Indian boys (one of whom is lost to history and one of whom died as a teenager)—and were guardians of eight other children.

26. Rohrbough, *The Trans-Appalachian Frontier*, 391-392.

27. President Donald Trump was mocked for saying something very much like this. But, even if he expressed himself awkwardly (on Twitter), he was right in spirit; his critics were wrong.

28. Parton, *Life of Andrew Jackson* 1: 113.

29. T. S. Eliot, London, to Allen Tate, 27 November 1930, in the Allen Tate Papers (C0106), Box 19, Folder 53, Princeton University.

30. Paul Johnson, *The Birth of the Modern* (New York: HarperCollins, 1991). Quotes are both from page 910.

31. Daniel Walker Howe, *What Hath God Wrought: The Transformation of America, 1815-1848* (New York: Oxford University Press, 2007), 328.

32. Howe, *What Hath God Wrought*, 105.

33. Ibid., 347, 357.

34. Ibid., 423.

35. President Donald Trump, "Remarks by the President on the 250th Anniversary of the Birth of President Andrew Jackson," May 15,

2017, delivered at The Hermitage, Nashville, Tennessee. Speech accessed at whitehouse.gov.

36.   Robert W. Merry, "Andy Jackson's Populism," *The American Conservative* 16 (May/June 2017), 23-27.

37.   Ibid.

Chapter Two: Republican Violence

1.   On the four great waves of migration to America, 1620-1775, see David Hackett Fischer, *Albion's Seed* (New York: Oxford University Press, 1989).

2.   Remini, *Life of Andrew Jackson*, 5.

3.   Parton, *Life of Andrew Jackson* 1: 58.

4.   See, for example, Tracy M. Kegley, "James White Stephenson: Teacher of Andrew Jackson," *Tennessee Historical Quarterly* 7 (March 1948): 38-51.

5.   Parton, *Life of Andrew Jackson*, 1:64.

6.   Ibid., 1:68.

7.   Quoted in Remini, *Andrew Jackson: The Course of American Empire, 1767-1821* (Baltimore, MD: The Johns Hopkins Press University Press, 1998), 11.

8.   John H. Eaton and John Reid, *The Life of Andrew Jackson* (1817; Philadelphia, PA: Samuel F. Bradford, 1824), 10. In a letter to George Bancroft, Jackson claimed this book to be the most accurate about his early life. See AJ to George Bancroft, December 9, 1841, in *Correspondence of Andrew Jackson* 6: 128.

9.   AJ to Andrew Jackson Donelson, *Papers of Andrew Jackson* 5: 163.

10.   Parton, *Life of Andrew Jackson* 1:69.

11.   Remini, *Life of Andrew Jackson*, 8.

12. Jackson, "Description of His Experiences During and Immediately Following the Revolutionary War," in *Papers of Andrew Jackson* 1: 5.

13. Parton, *Life of Andrew Jackson* 1:89.

14. This, according to Francis Blair. See Goff, "Physical Description," 305.

15. Jackson, "Description of His Experiences," in *Papers of Andrew Jackson* 1:7.

16. Jackson, "Description of His Experiences During and Immediately Following the Revolutionary War," in *Papers of Andrew Jackson* 1: 5-6. This remembrance is critical to an understanding of the Jacksons during the war.

17. Parton, *Life of Andrew Jackson* 1: 93.

18. Jackson, "Description of His Experiences," in *Papers of Andrew Jackson* 1:7.

19. Parton, *Life of Andrew Jackson* 1: 94-95.

20. Ibid., 1:89.

21. Jackson, "Description," in *Papers of Andrew Jackson* 1:7.

22. Notice of Law Licenses in North Carolina and Tennessee, in *Papers of Andrew Jackson* 1:10, 13.

23. Quoted in Reda C. Goff, "A Physical Profile of Andrew Jackson," *Tennessee Historical Quarterly* 28 (Fall 1969): 303.

24. Goff, "A Physical Profile," 303.

25. Andrew Jackson to Waightstill Avery, August 10, 1788, in Remini, *Life of Andrew Jackson*, 14-15.

26. Remini, *Life of Andrew Jackson*, 15.

27. Andrew Jackson to John Sevier, May 10, 1797, in *Papers of Andrew Jackson* 1: 141.

28. Andrew Jackson to John McNairy, May 12, 1797, in *Papers of Andrew Jackson* 1: 144.

29. Andrew Jackson to Willie Blount, February 21, 1798, in *Papers of Andrew Jackson* 1: 182.

30. See various letters and bills of sale, *Papers of Andrew Jackson* 1: 12-17.

31. Appointment, October 8, 1791, in *Papers of Andrew Jackson* 1: 29; and Commission, September 10, 1792, in *Papers of Andrew Jackson* 1: 37-38.

32. "Marriage Bond," March 1, 1785, in Appendix II, *Papers of Andrew Jackson* 1: 423.

33. "Permission for Robards to Sue for Divorce," December 20, 1790, in *Papers of Andrew Jackson* 1: 424.

34. "Public Writ Announcing Divorce Proceedings," January 24, 1792, in *Papers of Andrew Jackson* 1: 427.

35. Several legal testimonies offered in the 1820s assert that Robards had been abusive in the extreme, Rachel virtuous, and Rachel and Andrew chaste. See the various depositions quoted in *Papers of Andrew Jackson* 6: 240-241, fn 1-2.

36. Parton, *Life of Andrew Jackson* 1: 169.

37. George Cochran to Andrew Jackson, October 21, 1791, in *The Papers of Andrew Jackson* 1: 32.

38. "Marriage Bond—Andrew Jackson and Rachel Donelson Robards," January 17, 1794, in *Papers of Andrew Jackson* 1: 428; and "Marriage License," January 18, 1794, in *Papers of Andrew Jackson* 1: 44.

39. Charles Hammond, *A View of General Jackson's Domestic Relations* (no publisher listed, 1828).

40. Andrew Jackson to Rachel Jackson, May 9, 1796, in *The Papers of Andrew Jackson* 1: 91.

41. Because of a fire, very few of Rachel Donelson Jackson's letters survive. The ones that remain can be found throughout the several volumes of the *Papers of Andrew Jackson*. Additionally, Avery O.

Craven collected and edited a number of letters extant at the Huntington Library, San Marino, California. See Craven, "Letters of Andrew Jackson," *The Huntington Library Bulletin* 3 (February 1933): 109-134.

42. Parton, *Life of Andrew Jackson* 1: 211-212.

43. John Sevier, "Certificate of Election to the United States Senate, October 19, 1797, in *Papers of Andrew Jackson* 1: 150.

44. Andrew Jackson to Robert Hays, in *Papers of Andrew Jackson* 1: 152.

45. 45

46. 46

47. 47

48. Jackson to John Sevier, February 24, 1797, in *Papers of Andrew Jackson* 1: 126.

49. See various letters and documents, *Papers of Andrew Jackson* 1: 156ff.

50. Andrew Jackson to James Robertson, January 11, 1798, in *Papers of Andrew Jackson* 1: 164-165.

51. Joseph Anderson, Andrew Jackson, and William C.C. Claiborne to James McHenry, in *Papers of Andrew Jackson* 1: 181.

52. William Graham Sumner, *Andrew Jackson*, 10.

53. Quoted in Sumner, *Andrew Jackson*, 14; and in Parton, *Life of Andrew Jackson* 1: 219.

54. Quoted in Sumner, *Andrew Jackson*, 14.

55. Albert Gallatin to Walter Lowrie, May 22, 1824, in *Writings of Albert Gallatin* 2: 288-292.

56. Andrew Jackson to James Robertson, *Papers of Andrew Jackson* 1: 165.

57. Sumner, *Andrew Jackson*, 12.

58. Andrew Jackson to Robert Hays, *Papers of Andrew Jackson* 1: 173.

59. Andrew Jackson to John Donelson, January 18, 1798, in *Papers of Andrew Jackson* 1: 168.

60. Eaton and Reid, *Life of Andrew Jackson*, 18.

61. Jackson to Robert Hays, January 8, 1797, in *Papers of Andrew Jackson* 1: 111.

62. Andrew Jackson to Rachel Jackson, *Papers of Andrew Jackson* 1: 174.

63. Reid and Eaton, *Life of General Jackson*, 19.

64. Remini, *Life of Andrew Jackson*, 44.

65. See Grady McWhiney, *Cracker Culture: Celtic Ways in the Old South* (University of Alabama Press, 1988); and McWhiney and Forrest McDonald, "The South from Self-Sufficiency to Peonage: An Interpretation," *American Historical Review* 85 (1985).

66. Andrew Jackson to John Sevier, October 2, 1803, in *Papers of Andrew Jackson* 1: 367-368.

67. John Sevier, October 2, 1803, in *Papers of Andrew Jackson* 1: 368.

68. Andrew Jackson to the Public, October 10, 1803, in *Papers of Andrew Jackson* 1: 378-379.

69. Parton, *Life of Andrew Jackson* 1: 234-235.

70. Parton, *Life of Andrew Jackson* 1: 268-269.

71. Andrew Jackson to Charles Henry Dickinson, May 23, 1806, in *Papers of Andrew Jackson* 2: 98.

72. Parton, *Life of Andrew Jackson* 1: 299.

73. Parton, *Life of Andrew Jackson* 1: 301.

74. Statements of Hanson Catlet and Thomas Overton re: Duel, June 20, 1806, in *Papers of Andrew Jackson* 2: 104. For a report sympathetic to Dickinson, see "Nashville, June 7," *Hagerstown Maryland Herald and Weekly Advertiser* (July 11, 1806).

75. Andrew Jackson to Thomas Hart Benton, July 19, 1813, in *Papers of Andrew Jackson* 2: 413.

76. Thomas Hart Benton to Andrew Jackson, July 25, 1813, in *Papers of Andrew Jackson* 2: 415.

77. Thomas Hart Benton to the Public, September 10, 1813, in *Papers of Andrew Jackson* 2: 425.

Chapter Three: Frontiersman, Citizen Soldier, and Hero

1. See, for example, Washington Irving to Andrew Jackson, October 27, 1833, in Stanley T. Williams, "Washington Irving and Andrew Jackson," *Yale University Library Gazette* 19 (April 1945): 68.

2. Patricia Nelson Limerick, *The Legacy of Conquest* (New York: W.W. Norton, 1987).

3. Bruce Frohnen, "Revolutions, Not Made, But Prevented: 1776, 1688, and the Triumph of the Old Whigs," chapter in Gary L. Gregg II, ed., *Vital Remnants: America's Founding and the Western Tradition* (Wilmington, Del.: Intercollegiate Studies Institute, 1999), 281.

4. Andrew Jackson, "Toasts for Independence Day Celebration," July 1, 1805, in *Papers of Andrew Jackson* 2: 63.

5. Andrew Jackson to Willie Blount, February 15, 1810, in *Papers of Andrew Jackson* 2:237.

6. Ibid.

7. Andrew Jackson to the 2nd Division, March 7, 1812, in *Papers of Andrew Jackson* 2: 290-291.

8. Andrew Jackson to William Berkeley Lewis, March 13, 1813, in *Papers of Andrew Jackson* 2: 384-385.

9. Andrew Jackson to John Armstrong, March 15, 1813, in *Papers of Andrew Jackson* 2: 386.

10. Andrew Jackson to Thomas Jefferson, August 7, 1803, in *Papers of Andrew Jackson* 1: 354.

11. Andrew Jackson to George Washington Campbell, April 13, 1804, in *Papers of Andrew Jackson* 2: 16.

12. Andrew Jackson to Rachel Jackson, April 6, 1804, in *Papers of Andrew Jackson* 2: 13.

13. Andrew Jackson to John Coffee, April 28, 1804, in *Papers of Andrew Jackson* 2: 19.

14. Andrew Jackson to John McKee, January 30, 1793, in *Papers of Andrew Jackson* 1:40.

15. Andrew Jackson to John McKee, May 16, 1794, in *Papers of Andrew Jackson* 1:48-49.

16. Andrew Jackson to Rachel Jackson, December 29, 1813, in *Huntington Library Bulletin*, 115.

17. Andrew Jackson to William Henry Harrison, November 28, 1811, in *Papers of Andrew Jackson* 2: 270. For the best biographies of the Prophet and of Tecumseh, see the works of the extraordinary R. David Edmunds.

18. Andrew Jackson to Willie Blount, June 5, 1812, in *Papers of Andrew Jackson* 2: 301.

19. Felix Grundy, speech before the House, quoted in *Major Problems of in the Early Republic*, 156-57.

20. Andrew Jackson to Willie Blount, July 8, 1812, in *Papers of Andrew Jackson* 2: 311-313.

21. Willie Blount to Andrew Jackson, November 11, 1812, in *Papers of Andrew Jackson* 2: 338-339.

22. Andrew Jackson to Rachel Jackson, March 15, 1813, in *Papers of Andrew Jackson* 2: 387.

23. Ibid.

24. Reid and Eaton, *Life of General Jackson*, 26-27.

25. Reid and Eaton, *Life of General Jackson*, 23ff.; and Parton, *Life of Andrew Jackson* 1: 381.

26. Parton, *Life of Andrew Jackson* 1: 382.

27. Reid and Eaton, *Life of General Jackson*, 33; and Remini, *The Life of Andrew Jackson*.

28. Andrew Jackson to Thomas Pinckney, March 28, 1814, in *Gettysburg Adams Centinel* (April 27, 1814).

29. Remini, *The Life of Andrew Jackson*, 80-85.

30. Andrew Jackson to Willie Blount, April 18, 1814, in *Hagerstown Herald* (June 1, 1814).

31. Andrew Jackson to Rachel Jackson, December 29, 1813, in *Huntington Library Bulletin*, 113.

32. Andrew Jackson to Rachel Jackson, December 9, 1813, in *Huntington Library Bulletin*, 112-113.

33. Andrew Jackson to Rachel Jackson, March 4, 1814, in *Huntington Library Bulletin*, 115.

34. Resident of New Orleans quoted in Goff, "Physical Profile of Andrew Jackson," *Tennessee Historical Quarterly* 28 (Fall 1969), 303.

35. Andrew Jackson to Rachel Jackson, December 29, 1813, in *Huntington Library Bulletin*, 113-114.

36. Announcement in *Gettysburg Adams Centinel* (June 8, 1814); and Remini, *The Life of Andrew Jackson*, 84-85.

37. Andrew Jackson to Rachel Jackson, August 5, 1814, in *Huntington Library Bulletin*, 116-117. For the importance of New Orleans as a center of empire, see Bradley Folsom, *Arrendondo: Last Spanish Ruler of Texas and Northeastern New Spain* (Norman: University of Oklahoma Press, 2017), 71, 141-144, and 157.

38. Andrew Jackson to Rachel Jackson, August 5, 1814, in *Huntington Library Bulletin*, 116.

39. Andrew Jackson to Willie Blount, November 14, 1814, in "Two Uncollected Letters of Andrew Jackson," *Florida Historical Society Quarterly* 15 (January 1937): 170-171.

40. "Letters of John Innerarity: The Seizure of Pensacola by Andrew Jackson, November 7, 1814," *Florida Historical Society Quarterly* 9 (January 1931): 129.

41. "Glorious Victory," *The Maryland Herald* (February 15, 1815).

42. Johnson, *The Birth of the Modern*, 1-2.

43. "Glorious Victory," *The Maryland Herald* (February 15, 1815).

44. Andrew Jackson, "From New Orleans, January 19, 1815," *Hagerstown Herald* (February 15, 1815); and Remini, ed., "Andrew Jackson's Account of the Battle of New Orleans," *Tennessee Historical Quarterly* 26 (Spring 1967): 23-42.

45. See Paul Johnson, *The Birth of the Modern*, introduction.

46. "New Orleans," *Hagerstown Herald* (March 15, 1815).

Chapter Four: Conqueror and Hero

1. Remini, *The Life of Andrew Jackson*, 127.

2. Andrew Jackson to Mauricio de Zuniga, April 23, 1816, in *Papers of Andrew Jackson* 4: 22-23.

3. Mauricio de Zuniga to Andrew Jackson, May 26, 1816, in *Papers of Andrew Jackson* 4: 42-43.

4. Andrew Jackson to Rachel Jackson, May 29, 1817, in *Papers of Andrew Jackson* 4: 117.

5. James Monroe to Andrew Jackson, October 5, 1817, in *Papers of Andrew Jackson* 4: 48.

6. Andrew Jackson to James Monroe, December 20, 1817, in *Papers of Andrew Jackson* 4: 162.

7. John C. Calhoun to Andrew Jackson, December 26, 1817, in *Papers of Andrew Jackson* 4: 163.

8. Andrew Jackson, circular, January 11, 1818, in *Papers of Andrew Jackson* 4: 168-169.

9. Andrew Jackson to John C. Calhoun, January 27, 1818, in *Papers of Andrew Jackson* 4: 172-173.

10. Andrew Jackson to Francisco Caso y Luengo, April 6, 1818, in *Papers of Andrew Jackson* 4: 186; and Andrew Jackson to John C. Calhoun, April 8, 1818, in *Papers of Andrew Jackson* 4: 189-190.

11. Andrew Jackson to John C. Calhoun, May 5, 1818, in *Papers of Andrew Jackson* 4: 197-200.

12. "Louisiana," *Newport Mercury* (July 11, 1818); *Gettysburg Adam Centinel* (July 15, 1818); "American Papers," *London St. James Chronicle* (August 1, 1818); and "America," *London Star* (September 1, 1818).

13. Andrew Jackson to Jose Masot, May 23, 1818, in *Papers of Andrew Jackson* 4: 208-209.

14. Andrew Jackson to Rachel Jackson, June 2, 1818, in *Papers of Andrew Jackson* 4: 213.

15. James Monroe to Andrew Jackson, July 19, 1818, in *Papers of Andrew Jackson* 4: 224-226.

16. All of John Quincy Adams from John Quincy Adams, *Memoirs of John Quincy Adams* 4: 101-115.

17. Andrew Jackson to Richard Keith Call, August 5, 1818, in *Papers of Andrew Jackson* 4: 230; Andrew Jackson to John C. Calhoun, August 10, 1818, in *Papers of Andrew Jackson* 4: 231-233; and Andrew Jackson to James Monroe, August 19, 1818, in *Papers of Andrew Jackson* 4: 236-239.

18. Willie Blount to Andrew Jackson, April 18, 1819, in *Papers of Andrew Jackson* 4: 285.

19. Remini, *The Life of Andrew Jackson*, 127-128.

20. See *Papers of Andrew Jackson* 4: 300-305; and *Maryland Herald* (March 13, 1821).

21. Monroe asked Jackson to accept the position in a letter dated January 24, 1821. See James Monroe to Andrew Jackson, January 24, 1821, in *Papers of Andrew Jackson* 5: 9.

22. Andrew Jackson to James Monroe, February 11, 1821, in *Papers of Andrew Jackson* 5: 10.

23. Andrew Jackson to Andrew Jackson Donelson, March 31, 1821, in *Papers of Andrew Jackson* 5: 24.

24. Andrew Jackson to John Coffee, April 11, 1821, in *Papers of Andrew Jackson* 5: 28.

25. Andrew Jackson to John C. Calhoun, July 29, 1821, in *Papers of Andrew Jackson* 5: 86; and Andrew Jackson to James Jackson, August 2, 1821, in *Papers of Andrew Jackson* 5: 91-92.

26. Andrew Jackson, Proclamation to the Citizens of the Floridas, September 6, 1821, reprinted in *The Republican Compiler* (November 14, 1821).

27. Andrew Jackson, Proclamation to the Citizens of the Floridas, September 6, 1821, reprinted in *The Republican Compiler* (November 14, 1821).

28. Andrew Jackson to James C. Bronaugh, August 27, 1822, in Herbert J. Doherty, Jr., "Andrew Jackson on Manhood Suffrage, 1822," *Tennessee Historical Quarterly* 15 (March 1956): 60.

29. Andrew Jackson, Proclamation to the Citizens of the Floridas, September 6, 1821, reprinted in *The Republican Compiler* (November 14, 1821).

30. *London Morning Chronicle* (January 1, 1822).

31. Nomination reprinted in *London/St. James Chronicle* (October 3, 1822).

32. Gordon Wood, *The Radicalism of the American Revolution* (New York: Alfred A. Knopf, 1992), 365-66.

33. Warren, *History of the Revolution*, Vol. II, 644.

34. Jackson might not only have approved the "Letters of Wyoming" but might very well have offered suggestions to Eaton about what to write. See Andrew Jackson to William Berkeley Lewis, May 7, 1824, in *The Papers of Andrew Jackson*, 5: 404. See also, Robert P. Hay's excellent republican analysis of Wyoming, "The Case for Andrew Jackson in 1824: Eaton's *Wyoming Letters*," *Tennessee Historical Quarterly* 29 (Summer 1970): 139-40.

35. *Letters of Wyoming*, 4.

36. Ibid., 61.

37. Ibid., 94.

38. Quoted in *Letters of Wyoming*, 7.

39. *Letters of Wyoming*, 23.

40. Ibid.

41. Ibid., 64.

42. Ibid., 21.

43. Ibid., 62.

44. Ibid., 45

45. Ibid., 68.

46. Ibid., 69.

47. Ibid., 47.

48. Ibid., 26.

49. Ibid., 68.

50. Ibid., 69.

51. Ibid., 48.

52. Ibid., 24.

53. Ibid., 28.

54. Ibid., 56.

55. Ibid., 54.

56. Ibid., 61.

57. Ibid., 33.

58. Ibid., 89, 103.

Chapter Five: The Reluctant President

1.   Samuel Ragland Overton to Andrew Jackson, August 1, 1821, in
     Papers of Andrew Jackson 5:89.

2.   Andrew Jackson to James Gadsden, December 6, 1821, in *Papers
     of Andrew Jackson* 5: 121.

3.   Andrew Jackson to George Gibson, January 29, 1822, in *Papers of
     Andrew Jackson* 5: 139.

4.   Andrew Jackson to Richard Keith Call, June 29, 1822, in *Papers
     of Andrew Jackson* 5: 199.

5.   "General Jackson," *Maryland Herald* (October 28, 1823).
     Humorously, some London papers reported Andrew Jackson's
     return to the Senate in 1823 as his election to the U.S. presidency.
     See *London Morning Chronicle* (December 3, 1823).

6.   Andrew Jackson to John Overton, November 8, 1823, in Stanley
     F. Horn, ed., "Some Jackson-Overton Correspondence," *Tennessee
     Historical Quarterly* 6 (June 1947): 163

7.   Andrew Jackson to John Overton, December 5, 1823, in Horn,
     164.

8.   Remini, *Life of Andrew Jackson*, 148-149.

9.   "Julius Caesar and Andrew Jackson," *Terre-Haute Western
     Register and Advertiser* (October 18, 1823). See also, *Warren (PA)
     Gazette* (October 9, 1828). The opposition threw around such
     classical epitaphs at Jackson constantly. Sometimes he was Julius
     Caesar, sometimes he was Mark Antony, and, once, rather cleverly,
     he was Phaeton, the son of Zeus, killed by his father for driving a
     chariot recklessly. On Jackson as Phaeton, see *Adams Sentinel*
     (January 30, 1828).

10. "Military Chieftains," *Adams Sentinel* (October 22, 1828).

11. Clay's letter, printed in the *Richmond Enquirer*, February 8, 1825,
     quoted in *Papers of Andrew Jackson* 6: 34, fn1.

12. Andrew Jackson to Samuel Swartwout, February 22, 1825, in *Papers of Andrew Jackson* 6: 41.

13. Andrew Jackson to John Telemachus Johnson, October 30, 1825, in *Papers of Andrew Jackson* 6: 117.

14. "Jackson Meeting," *Hagerstown Torchlight and Republican Advertiser* (February 3, 1824). Not surprisingly, English papers did not much like the glorification of Jackson's military acumen. See, for example, *London New Times* (November 26, 1824).

15. Andrew Jackson to John Coffee, January 5, 1825, in *Papers of Andrew Jackson* 6: 6.

16. Andrew Jackson to John Coffee, January 23, 1825, in *Papers of Andrew Jackson* 6: 18.

17. *Diary of John Quincy Adams* 6: 447.

18. Ibid., 6: 464.

19. Ibid., 6: 469.

20. Ibid., 6: 474.

21. Ibid., 6: 483.

22. Ibid., 6: 508.

23. John Henry Eaton to John Overton, February 7, 1825, in *Papers of Andrew Jackson* 6: 26.

24. In my own research on the events surrounding South Carolina's secession and the Major Anderson's move to Fort Sumter in late December 1826, I have found Buchanan telling one side one thing, while telling another side something completely different, all within a matter of days. That Buchanan lied cannot be doubted. While all lies are terrible, Buchanan's lies in late 1860 and early 1861 had dire consequences, serving as a catalyst for the American Civil War. For the letters to, from, and about Buchanan and the Corrupt Bargain, see multiple letters in *The Papers of Andrew Jackson*, vol. 6. For Clay's take on the matter and defense of his own position, see Henry Clay, "To the Public," June 29, 1827, in *Hagerstown*

Torchlight (July 19, 1827). For Buchanan's, see "Mr. Buchanan's Letter," August 8, 1827, in *Hagerstown Torchlight* (August 16, 1827). Buchanan was not the only future president mixed up in the "Corrupt Bargain." See, for example, public letter of William Henry Harrison, November 5, 1827, in *Hagerstown Torchlight* (November 29, 1827).

25. *London New Times* (March 16, 1825).

26. Andrew Jackson to William Berkeley Lewis, January 29, 1825, in *Papers of Andrew Jackson* 6: 22-23.

27. Andrew Jackson to John Overton, February 10, 1825, in *Papers of Andrew Jackson* 6: 28.

28. Andrew Jackson to William Berkeley Lewis, in *Papers of Andrew Jackson* 6: 29-30.

29. Samuel Swartwout to Andrew Jackson, February 18, 1825, in *Papers of Andrew Jackson* 6: 32-34.

30. Andrew Jackson to John Coffee, October 30, 1825, in *Papers of Andrew Jackson* 6: 115; and Andrew Jackson to Samuel Swartwout, December 15, 1825, in *Papers of Andrew Jackson* 6: 126.

31. On Pennsylvania's nomination, see James Buchanan to Andrew Jackson, March 8, 1826, in *Papers of Andrew Jackson* 6: 147.

32. Andrew Jackson to John Overton and the Citizens of Nashville," April 16, 1825, in *Papers of Andrew Jackson* 6: 62-63.

33. Andrew Jackson to Henry Lee, October 7, 1825, in *Papers of Andrew Jackson* 6: 104-105. See also, Andrew Jackson to William Berkeley Lewis, February 20, 1825, in *Papers of Andrew Jackson* 6: 36.

34. In November 1827, a Gettysburg, Pennsylvania, newspaper correctly noted that the two old parties had "so strangely blended together," that no label meant anything. See *Gettysburg Sentinel* (November 21, 1827).

35. On a local Democratic Party opposing Jackson, see *Adams Sentinel* (January 30, 1828). On the names of parties supporting Jackson, see, for example, *Wilmington American Watchman* (February 15, 1828). By 1830, no permanent name existed. See, for example, "The Federal Jacksonians," *Hagerstown Mail* (April 9, 1830).

36. David Crockett to C.D. McLean, March 5, 1830, in *Washington National Intelligencer* (April 22, 1830).

37. Glyndon G. Van Deusen offered a nice synopsis of the first decade of the Democratic Party's existence in his *The Jacksonian Era, 1828-1848* (New York: Harper & Row, 1959). As he argued, the party did not take shape until the middle of Jackson's second administration.

38. Donald B. Cole, *The Presidency of Andrew Jackson* (Lawrence: University Press of Kansas, 1993), 213-214, 245-254.

39. "On Debates in Congress," May 3, 1825, *Gales and Seaton's Register*, 671.

40. "John Randolph," quoted in *Adams Sentinel* (April 30, 1828).

41. John Henry Eaton to Andrew Jackson, January 27, 1827, in *Papers of Andrew Jackson* 6: 267-268.

42. John Henry Eaton to Andrew Jackson, March 4, 1828, in *Papers of Andrew Jackson* 6: 429-430. On opposition papers doing everything possible to rouse Jackson to reveal his violent temper, see "Villanous [sic]," *Delaware Patriot* (July 29, 1828).

43. John Overton, "Vindication of General Jackson," *Washington Intelligencer* (May 17, 1827).

44. "Address to Fellow Citizens," May 22, 1827, in *Gettysburg Republican Compiler* (June 6, 1827).

45. Even in an age of slavery, slave traders were considered the lowest of the low white society. On the accusation of Jackson as slave trader, see *Indianapolis Journal* (October 9, 1828); and *Hagerstown*

Torchlight (October 23, 1828). On his ties to Burr, see, for example, "Burr Conspiracy," *Hagerstown Torchlight* (October 16, 1828).

46. *Washington Intelligencer* (August 13, 1827).

47. *Washington Intelligencer* (July 8, 1828). For another good—meaning honest and well-written—attack on Jackson, see *Adams Sentinel* (October 1, 1828). While the *Intelligencer* almost always maintained its dignity, the *Adams Sentinel* rarely did, which makes this piece all the more interesting.

48. *Hagerstown Torchlight* (December 13, 1827).

49. *Hagerstown Torchlight* (July 10, 1828).

50. See "Rank Villainy and Obscenity," *Hagerstown Mail* (August 16, 1828); and "Gen. Jackson 76," *Delaware Weekly Advertiser* (August 7, 1828).

51. Andrew Jackson to R.K. Call, August 16, 1828, in *Virginia Historical Magazine* 29 (April 1921): 191-192.

Chapter Six: The World Is Governed Too Much

1. See, for example, Parton, *The Life of Andrew Jackson* 1: 107-108.

2. Andrew Jackson to Governor William Rabun, May 7, 1818, in *Papers of Andrew Jackson* 4: 202.

3. Andrew Jackson to Katherine Duane Morgan, January 3, 1828, in *Papers of Andrew Jackson* 7: 5.

4. Andrew Jackson to William Polk, January 5, 1829, in *Papers of Andrew Jackson* 7: 7.

5. Andrew Jackson to Mary Middleton Rutledge Fogg, January 17, 1829, in *Papers of Andrew Jackson* 7: 14

6. Obituary of Rachel Jackson, *Nashville Republican*, quoted in *Hagerstown Mail* (January 9, 1829).

7. Amos Kendall to Jane Kendall, January 15, 1829, in *Autobiography of Amos Kendall* (Boston: Lee and Shepard, 1872), 279.

8. *Adams Sentinel* (January 21, 1829).

9. *Hagerstown Mail* (February 13, 1829).

10. A constant theme of both of his administrations was to identify and root out any corruption at any level of the government. See, for example, Albert Somit, "Some Sidelights Upon Jacksonian Administration," *Mississippi Valley Historical Review* 35 (June 1948): 91-98.

11. Andrew Jackson, Message to Congress, December 8, 1829.

12. *Hagerstown Torchlight* (May 27, 1830).

13. Cole, *Presidency of Andrew Jackson*, 26ff.

14. Martin Van Buren, *Autobiography*, ed. by John C. Fitzpatrick (Washington D.C.: American Historical Association, 1920), 231.

15. Andrew Jackson to John Henry Eaton, August 3, 1830, in *Papers of Andrew Jackson* 7: 462.

16. Andrew Jackson to Susan Wheeler Decatur, January 2, 1830, in *Papers of Andrew Jackson* 7: 5.

17. Cole, *The Presidency of Andrew Jackson*, 85.

18. Ibid., 86.

19. Amos Kendall to Jane Kendall (Amos's second wife), January 15, 1829, in *Autobiography*, 280.

20. Kendall, *Autobiography*, 293.

21. Ibid., 290.

22. Ibid., 297.

23. Ibid., 301.

24. See, for example, Charles Grier Sellers, Jr., "Andrew Jackson versus the Historians," *Mississippi Valley Historical Review* 44 (March 1958): 621-622.

25. Kendall, *Autobiography*, 298.

26. Kendall, *Autobiography*, 309.

27. Kendall, *Autobiography*, 319-320.

28. Francis Paul Prucha, S.J., "Andrew Jackson's Indian Policy: A Reassessment," *Journal of American History* 56 (December 1969): 527. See also his earlier work, "Indian Removal and the Great American Desert," *Indiana Magazine of History* 59 (December 1963): 299-322; and his later work, "The Challenge of Indian History," *Journal of the West* 34 (January 1995). For a more neutral examination of Jackson's Indian policy, see Ronald N. Satz, "Jackson and the Indians," *Tennessee Historical Quarterly* 38 (Summer 1979): 158-166.

29. On the Jeffersonian view of the American Indian, see Bernard W. Sheehan, *Seeds of Extinction: Jeffersonian Philanthropy and the American Indian* (University of North Carolina Press, 1973).

30. Andrew Jackson, Message to Congress, December 8, 1829.

31. The "Permanent Indian Frontier" was a jagged line of forts running from present-day Minnesota to Louisiana, lasting from 1817 to 1848. Among the forts were Jesup, Washita, Towson, Smith, Gibson, Scott, Leavenworth, Atkinson, and Snelling. The area west of these forts, most Americans believed, was the "Great American Desert," unsuitable for English-style yeoman agriculture. The Indians, especially those removed from east of the Missouri River, could live there in peace, unharmed by whites, and able to advance culturally, at least as Jeffersonian theory went.

32. Andrew Jackson, Message to Congress, December 8, 1829. The drafts of this message, with the important contributions by John Eaton and Martin Van Buren, can be found in *Papers of Andrew Jackson* 7: 601-630.

33. "The Indian Bill," *Washington National Intelligencer* (May 27, 1830).

34. Alexis De Tocqueville, *Democracy in America* vol. 2 (4 volume Liberty Fund edition).

35. See Bradley J. Birzer, "'An appearance of lively industry about the place': Choctaw Economic Success in Indian Territory, 1831-1861," *Continuity: A Journal of History* 24 (Autumn 2000).

36. Tocqueville, *Democracy in America*, vol. 2.

37. Remini, *Andrew Jackson*, 179

38. *The Globe* quoted in Remini, *The Life of Andrew Jackson*, 201.

39. Alexis de Tocqueville, *Democracy in America*, ed. by J.P. Mayer (New York: Harper Collins, 1969), 513. The best single study examining Jacksonian associationalism is Don Harrison Doyle, *The Social Order of a Frontier Community: Jacksonville, Illinois, 1825-1870* (Champagne: University of Illinois, 1983). Robert Wiebe also deals with this theme, but rather cynically, in his *Self Rule: A Cultural History of American Democracy* (Chicago: University of Chicago Press, 1996). On Jacksonian political economy, see Lawrence H. White, ed., *Democratick Editorials: Essays in Jacksonian Political Economy* by William Leggett (Indianapolis: Liberty Fund, 1984).

40. Andrew Jackson to John Overton, May 13, 1830, in *Papers of Andrew Jackson* 8: 261.

41. Andrew Jackson, veto, in *Papers of Andrew Jackson* 7: 280-282. On Jackson's economic language, see Joseph Dorfman, "The Jackson Wage-Earner Thesis," *American Historical Review* 54 (January 1949): 296-306; Edward Pessen, "Society and Politics in the Jacksonian Era," *The Register of the Kentucky Historical Society* 82 (Winter 1984): 1-27; and Daniel Feller, "Toward a Jacksonian Synthesis," *Journal of the Early Republic* 10 (Summer 1990): 135-161.

42. *Hagerstown Torchlight* (June 17, 1830).

43. Quoted in Remini, *The Life of Andrew Jackson*, 272.

44. Andrew Jackson, Bank Message, July 10, 1832.

45. Ibid. For a good assessment and summation of the arguments against and for Jackson's veto, see Michael Holt, *Rise and Fall of the American Whig Party* (New York: Oxford University Press, 2003), 16ff.

46. John Randolph of Roanoke to Andrew Jackson, March 11, 1832, in *Papers of Andrew Jackson* 10: 161.

47. See, for example, Paul McGouldrick, "How Jacksonians Favored Industrialization," *Reason Papers* 10 (Spring 1985): 17-32; and Robert Whaples, "Were Andrew Jackson's Policies Good for the Economy?" *Independent Review* 18 (Spring 2014): 545-558.

Chapter Seven: Nullifying the Nullifiers

1. Speech of Daniel Webster, January 26-27, 1830, in *Webster-Hayne Debate*, 143-144.

2. Andrew Jackson, Toast, April 13, 1830, in *Papers of Andrew Jackson* 8: 190.

3. John Randolph of Roanoke to Andrew Jackson, March 18, 1832, in *Papers of Andrew Jackson* 10: 177.

4. Ibid.

5. The Declaration and the Articles of Confederation are reprinted in George W. Carey and James McClellan, eds., *The Federalist by Alexander Hamilton, John Jay, and James Madison* (Indianapolis, Ind.: Liberty Fund, 2001), pg. 498 and pg. 500 respectively.

6. McDonald, *States' Rights and the Union*, 11.

7. Ibid., 15-16.

8. Ibid., 20-21.

9. Ibid., 22.

10. Quoted in George Brown Tindall and David E. Shi, *America: A Narrative History*, 5th ed. (New York: W. W. Norton, 1999), 411.

11. Quoted in George Dangerfield, *The Awakening of American Nationalism: 1815–1828* (New York: Harper & Row, 1965), 18.

12. Andrew Jackson to John C. Calhoun, May 13, 1830, in *Papers of Andrew Jackson* 8: 256.

13. John C. Calhoun to Andrew Jackson, May 29, 1830, in *Papers of Andrew Jackson* 8: 305-321.

14. Andrew Jackson to John C. Calhoun, May 30, 1830, in *Papers of Andrew Jackson* 8: 322.

15. Calhoun, *A Disquisition on Government*.

16. Ibid.

17. Ibid.

18. Ibid.

19. Ibid.

20. Ibid.

21. Ibid.

22. Ibid.

23. Ibid.

24. Ibid.

25. Jackson offered an honest assessment of the progress of his actions against the nullifiers in a letter to his old friend and political ally, Nathaniel Macon. See, Andrew Jackson to Nathaniel Macon, September 2, 1833, in *Correspondence of Andrew Jackson* 5: 176. Macon disagreed with Jackson's actions, but still considered him an honorable and loyal republican.

26. Andrew Jackson to Rev. Andrew J. Crawford, May 1, 1833, in *Correspondence of Andrew Jackson* 5: 72.

27. Andrew Jackson to Martin Van Buren, January 13, 1833, in *Correspondence of Andrew Jackson* 5: 3.

28. Andrew Jackson to Joel Poinsett, January 24, 1833, in *Correspondence of Andrew Jackson* 5: 11.

29.   Andrew Jackson to Rev. Hardy M. Cryer, February 20, 1833, in
      Correspondence of Andrew Jackson 5: 19.

Chapter Eight: True Republican, True American, and True Heir

1.   Martin Van Buren to Andrew Jackson, July 22, 1834, in
      Correspondence of Andrew Jackson 5: 274.
2.   Andrew Jackson to Commodore J.D. Elliott, March 27, 1845, in
      "An Andrew Jackson Letter," *Register of the Kentucky State
      Historical Society* 11 (September 1913): 63.

Index